NORTHERN LOVE

NORTHERN LOVE

An Exploration of Canadian Masculinity

Paul Nonnekes

AU PRESS

Cultural Dialectics series

© 2008 Paul Nonnekes

Published by AU Press, Athabasca University
1200, 10011 – 109 Street
Edmonton, AB T5J 3S8

Library and Archives Canada Cataloguing in Publication

Nonnekes, Paul, 1961-
Northern love : an exploration of Canadian masculinity / Paul Nonnekes.

(Cultural dialectics)
Also available in electronic format.
ISBN 978-1-897425-22-0

1. Masculinity – Canada. 2. Masculinity – Social aspects–Canada. 3. Love –
Psychological aspects. 4. Hood, Robert (Fictitious character). 5. Peek
(Fictitious character). 6. Wiebe, Rudy, 1934- – Characters – Robert Hood.
7. Kroetsch, Robert, 1927- – Characters – Peek. 8. Masculinity in literature.
9. Love in literature. I. Title. II. Series: Cultural dialectics series (Print)

HQ1090.7.C2N65 2008   305.310971   C2008-902808-2

Printed and bound in Canada by Marquis Book Printing

Book design by Infoscan Collette, Québec

Cover design and illustration by Rod Michalchuk, General Idea

TABLE OF CONTENTS

INTRODUCTION

There has been quite a bit of discussion lately in Canada about our relationship to the North. One of those discussions involves the issue of Arctic sovereignty. With the warming temperatures and increased melting of the polar ice cap, reference is made to the Northwest Passage as a viable route for shipping and thus to whether Canada has political sovereignty over northern waters. Another prominent topic has been the enormous resource wealth in the North and the economic prosperity that those resources might bring. If the first decades of the twentieth century saw the focus of Canada shift to the West, it seems that in the first decades of the twenty-first century we are witnessing a shift in focus to the North. To paraphrase Robert Kroetsch (1995), if the earlier injunction was "go West," now the injunction is "go North."

This work complies with Kroetsch's injunction to go North. My desire, though, is not to explore the issues of political sovereignty or resource wealth but instead to explore the much different issue of love. The issue of love has not been front and centre in the recent discussions of the Canadian North, but I believe that it is a very significant element that needs serious attention. Political sovereignty and resource wealth may be important issues for Canadians, but I would contend that the issue of love is as well. In a sense, I am calling for the debate on the North to be expanded somewhat beyond issues of political control and economic power and to encompass the complex bonds and desires that tie humans together in what we often refer to as love.

What I mean by 'love' will emerge as the analysis in the book progresses, but let me say that when I refer to the importance of love, and in this case a distinctively northern love, I am referring to love in a gendered sense. More specifically, I am referring to the love of the mother and the love of the father. My analysis will explore the distinctiveness of a maternal and a paternal northern love. And the analysis narrows itself once more in a gendered way, because my intent is to explore maternal and paternal love in relation to the specific experience of Canadian men and the influence of masculine ideals on their lives. This book, then, will explore in some depth the relationship between northern love and Canadian masculinity.

In order to understand better the rationale for focusing on Canadian masculinity within the context of maternal and paternal love, it may be helpful to return to the West-North contrast for a moment and overlay the American-Canadian contrast. Michael Kimmel, in his social-historical work on American manhood (1996), claims that the American push to the West was an attempt by men to escape cultural feminization, a feminization associated with a male who had become far too domesticated. The escape from the maternal domestic scene and the feminized home led, according to Kimmel, to a reaffirmation of a particular kind of oedipal frontier male, virile, uncontained, and proudly violent (see also Bosso, McCall, and Garceau 2001). Kimmel believes that this western frontier masculinity has had and continues to have an enormous influence on the identities of American men.

If it is true that a reassertion of oedipal masculinity and a fear of cultural feminization are important characteristics of the movement of American men West then what can we say about the movement of Canadian men North? If there is a strong American cultural ideal of the West that says that men who love can only do so through fear of a love that comes through the maternal domesticated home, does this same relation to love hold for Canadian men who move North, or do Canadian men who move North present us with a different conception of love and a different relationship to the maternal domesticated home? And what kind of paternal ideal emerges for Canadian men who move North as they negotiate a distinctive relationship with the maternal? The intent of this book is to try and answer these questions by situating them within the overall context of northern love.

Another approach in beginning to understand the importance of the North for Canadian men and Canadian masculinity is to think of Canada as a northern nation. In her wonderfully crafted book,

Canada and the Idea of North (2002), Sherrill Grace refers to her "desire to understand this stubborn, complex, infuriating place called home." (xii) In pursuing her quest she asks "how the *here* called Canada has been constructed, represented, and articulated." (xi, xii, italics in text) Grace, though, believes that to understand Canada we must look North. She says:

> [I]t seems to me that now, more than ever before, it is impor-
> tant for Canadians to look North and in looking North to
> celebrate the creation of Nunavut, to appreciate the depen-
> dence of the South on Canada's Northern resources, to recog-
> nize the crucial role we must play in safeguarding an Arctic
> environment and in articulating policies for a circumpolar
> world. (xii)

According to Grace, in order to meet the challenges of the future, we as Canadians need to "come to terms with how we got here from there when there ... was also defined as North." (xi) She is thus led to investigate what she believes are various important "ideas" of the North that are represented in writing, painting, music, and film.

Take the example of "writing the North." (Part 2) Grace refers to Northrop Frye's *The Bush Garden* as important in establishing a tradition where the North is seen as a "sinister and menacing monster" which evokes "stark terror." (Frye in Grace, 32) This evocation of terror is accompanied by a mystical vision of the North "as pure but overwhelmingly white, silent, and spiritual as *opposed* to material or bodily presence." (33) From Frye in the late 1960s to Margot Northey (*The Haunted Wilderness*) in the 1970s, to Allison Mitcham (*The Northern Imagination*) and Ann Davis (*A Distant Harmony*) in the 1980s, to Margaret Atwood (*Strange Things)* in the 1990s, we can "trace a critical construction of a deadly, inhuman North character-ized by mystery, danger and adventure...." (33)

Grace also has a chapter in her book entitled "Fictions of the North" (chapter 5) in which she highlights the work of Rudy Wiebe and Robert Kroetsch. She emphasizes that "together with Robert Kroetsch, he [Wiebe] identifies himself categorically with the North and with Northern narratives of Nation." (186) Grace's reference to the importance of Wiebe and Kroetsch was significant in the conception of this book and my decision to concentrate on their work, in particular their work on the North.

———◦•⊰———

This idea of Canada as a northern nation is explored by Wiebe in his essay "Exercising Reflection," which forms the lead article in his collection *Playing Dead: A Contemplation Concerning the Arctic* (1989). Wiebe's essay can be seen as setting the reflective ground for his later imaginative explorations of love in the novel *A Discovery of Strangers* (1994), which will be analyzed in detail in Section One of this book. In the essay "Exercising Reflection," Wiebe refers to the distinctive northern experience of borders and boundaries. He tells us that, after having flown over Canada many times, "I have become convinced that the only natural human boundary is water." (1989, 9) When we think of borders in Canada, we often think of our southern border with the United States. According to Wiebe, this border is geographically artificial because it is not defined by water.

This does not seem to be true of our northern border, however. Wiebe tells us that "when you stand on the sand of Darnley Bay or on the ice ridge pressured up the beach of Kittizazuit, the boundary of Canada is nothing if not absolute.... The water declares it." (10) This northern perspective is quickly complicated as Wiebe considers the relationship between ocean and river. Standing at the edge of Canada on the shores of the Arctic Ocean, he wonders, "where does the ocean begin and where do the rivers end?" (10)

The importance of this question is reinforced for Wiebe by an experience in a small boat moving through the ocean fog. They are trying to find the Hornaday River, and although the owner of the boat assures Wiebe that they are moving toward the river, his eyes tell him nothing. He sees only "angry water ... vicious waves breaking against the edge of the boat." (10, 11) Then suddenly the engine of the boat is cut and the owner declares to him that they are no longer in the ocean, but on the river. Yet, Wiebe remains confused: "The waves and shoals looked the same, the fog which destroyed not only perspective but eliminated all horizon seemed exactly the same." (11) There was one subtle difference, though: the water was not salty. This leads Wiebe to ask whether the only sensory indication that they had entered the river was that it tasted different.

We often say that when we move from the ocean to the river we are moving inland. Wiebe responds:

But 'inland' is a convenient chimera, a mythological beast
concocted by our refusal to imagine and thereby to understand.
Though we ordinarily think the rivers run from the heights of
land and mountains to eventually vanish in the sea, when you
approach a river from the ocean it becomes more enlightening
to recognize that rivers are the gnarled fresh fingers of the sea
reaching for the mountains. (12)

As he writes, Wiebe is sitting in his office overlooking the North
Saskatchewan River. Influenced by the perspective that moves from
North to South, he concludes that the North Saskatchewan River is
one small tentacle of "the Circumpolar Sea ... that great global sea
which surrounds us and in so doing defines our true boundaries."
(13) If this is true, if the tentacles of the northern ocean are stretched
out through the land called Canada, then "it is both philosophically
proper and imaginatively pleasing that the first whites to explore the
Canadian Arctic tundra and its coast were sailors." (13)

Wiebe's reflections about the importance of the northern landscape provide inspiration for his novel *A Discovery of Strangers*
(1994), which charts the journey of the sailors of the first Franklin
Expedition through northern Canada. The novel explores the contact
between the men of the Expedition and the Tetsot'ine Indians of the
Yellowknife region. It seems that the strong consideration of Canada
as a northern nation defined by a northern landscape leads, by a kind
of force of desire, to the question of northern love. It is as if Wiebe's
own travels through the North of Canada led him to think of love.
Landscape and love go together hand in hand. They are intimately
intertwined, such that consideration of one leads to consideration of
the other. They are in partnership. By writing this novel, Wiebe seems
to be telling us that the partnership that develops between the English
sailors and the northern landscape cannot be properly understood
without a strong consideration of the partnership that develops
between these sailors and the Tetsot'ine Indians. Especially the partnership of love. This is why the novel focuses its attention on the love
affair between Robert Hood, one of the officers on the Expedition,
and Greenstockings, a young Tetsot'ine woman.

There are three episodes in the story Wiebe tells that I would
like to highlight and reflect upon in Section One of this book. The
first episode involves the relationship between Hood and the shaman
Keskarrah, and principally Keskarrah teaching Hood how to see and

draw. The second is the emerging love affair between Hood and Greenstockings. The third is Hood's tragic death out on the barrens.

In these three episodes we witness an unravelling of English masculinity. What kind of unravelling? Is it the same as the unravelling that dominates the American experience, one where there is a return to a dominating and violent masculinity? My thesis will be that, at least in the imagination of Wiebe, the encounter of the English sailors with the northern frontier, and the Aboriginal people living there, leads to a distinctive encounter with the presence of the father in both imaginary and oedipal forms, and that this encounter with two fathers occurs through a dramatic encounter with the love of the mother. In Wiebe's telling, it is this playing out of maternal love in relation to paternal love that is at the heart of the drama of love. You could even say that maternal love in relation to paternal love is the distinctive experience of masculinity on the Canadian frontier, the distinctive experience of northern love.

There are five theoretical issues that I address in Section One. These theoretical issues will be approached in the context of contemporary debates in psychoanalysis and social theory.

The first theoretical issue in Section One concerns the relationship between naming and seeing. In the context of Wiebe's novel, I attempt to make sense of the unravelling of the English name and the encounter with the Tetsot'ine image. The men of the English Expedition seek to name everything in the North, the rivers, the lakes, the hills, the rocks. Yet this naming is quickly troubled and the English find that they are heavily reliant, for their very survival in the North, on the ability of the Tetsot'ine, especially, the shaman Keskarrah, to access images of the land – images that, for example, tell where the caribou are travelling and where the esker of trees for shelter might lie.

My contention will be that it is the unravelling of the English word that allows an affective transfer back to images of the mother. I turn to the work of psychoanalytic theorist Kaja Silverman in *World Spectators* (2000), where she tries to bring Lacan and Heidegger together by turning back to Freud's work on the image. Silverman argues that the word is more bound to the ego and its quest to keep pleasure constant (and thus under control), whereas the image allows for an increase in pleasure (that can be very disturbing for the ego) and, subsequently, an affective transfer to new experiences. My argument will be that one of the fundamental encounters in the North is the encounter of the English word with the Aboriginal image.

This is especially true in the experience of Robert Hood, who is a sketcher on the Expedition. Hood wants to draw Greenstockings, and, as this desire to draw her image unfolds we find him increasingly moving into the imagined world of the maternal. The question for Hood's masculinity is what relation this affective transfer back to the imagined world of the maternal has with his ongoing struggle with the love of the father.

The second theoretical issue in Section One involves interpretations of the master-slave relationship. The English of the Franklin Expedition readily see themselves as masters in relation to the original inhabitants of the land. I make use of Judith Butler's (1997) provocative reading of the master-slave relationship in Hegel to argue for an overcoming of the positions of master and slave, such that the subject considered slave ultimately has the means for productive transformation. In the context of Wiebe's novel, I will argue that the original presentation of a master-English in relation to slave-Tetsot'ine slowly unravels and produces unexpected reversals.

The third theoretical issue in Section One explores the importance of the imaginary in the Lacanian triad of imaginary/symbolic/real. My argument will be that in Wiebe's novel we witness, especially in the figure of Robert Hood, a return to the real. A fuller explanation of the Lacanian concept of the real will be provided in the main body of this work, but we can say for now that the real refers to an order of being that escapes all symbolic conceptualization. A subject has access to the real through a special kind of object, what the Lacanians call *objet a* (literally, object of the other), but which I will refer to as a "strange" object. Ordinary objects are conceptualized within the normative forms provided by the culture and society in which we live. An encounter with strange objects tends to make ordinary conceptualization fail, and it is when ordinary conceptualization fails that the subject begins to experience the real.

There are, however, differing ways of understanding the relationship of the real to those two other important Lacanian registers, the imaginary and the symbolic. There is a common understanding of this relationship which I see represented in the work of Slavoj Žižek, one that privileges the relationship between the symbolic and the real with the connection to the imaginary seen primarily as an obstacle to be overcome. If we privilege the relationship to the real through the *objet a*, then for Žižek, the encounter with *objets a* occurs principally in the symbolic register. The imaginary register, with its primarily narcissistic demand for ideal identification, will always thwart the revelatory power of the *objet a*. I turn to a critique of Žižek by Judith Butler (1993) which attempts to rescue the concept of the imaginary from the Lacanian critique. Butler sees the symbolic in the form of symbolic law as being an historically received normative order that thwarts resistance, and it is through imaginary ideals of lost possibilities (ones denied by the prevailing symbolic law) that strange objects are given the space to thrive.

My argument will be that Robert Hood is returned to the real through his encounter with strange objects of the imaginary, principally his encounter with Greenstockings, a young Aboriginal woman and her father, Keskarrah. This imaginary return to lost possibilities is significantly connected to Hood's experience of the paternal and the maternal. First, we have the failure of his Anglican priest father, who abandons him. This is an abandonment that causes Hood trauma, one could say a trauma of the real. Second, in the face of this traumatic encounter, we witness Hood re-experiencing the mother's love, an imaginary return to his mother in the kitchen of his English home, a return that is induced by his experience in the family lodge of Keskarrah, the Tetsot'ine shaman. Rather than a denial of the experience of hitting the real (which I presume would be Žižek's interpretation), I will interpret this movement of Hood back to the maternal as representing a productive relationship between the imaginary and the real.

The fourth theoretical issue in Section One concerns the question of gender and what I will refer to as the emergence of a strange gender. The relationship between Robert Hood and Greenstockings takes peculiar routes, and one effect of these routes is the unfolding of unstable and precarious gender identities for each, that rub against any normative understanding of masculine and feminine in our society. In order to flesh out the implications of this emergence of a strange gender, I will spend some time looking at Judith Butler's explorations of gender in her work *Antigone's Claim* (200). Against the grain of both Hegel's and Lacan's interpretations of the story of Antigone, Butler wishes to propose a reading that allows us to productively entertain alternative forms of gender construction that are able to consistently resist the norm. In working through the relationship of Hood and Greenstockings, I will propose that northern love invites the possibility of strange gender.

The fifth theoretical issue to be addressed in Section One concerns the relationship of love and trauma. Robert Hood both experiences intense love as he lies in the Keskarrah family lodge with Greenstockings and relives extreme trauma as he lies dying on the barrens.

There is a strong tradition in Lacanian psychoanalysis, especially the work of Žižek (2002), which argues that subjective destitution leads to a traumatic encounter with the real. What are the characteristics of Hood's particular form of subjective destitution? Wiebe presents a narrative wherein Hood's particular traumas originate in a lack of paternal love from his priest-father. If there is, in Hood's case, a strong relationship between trauma and the paternal, how does this relate to the experience of love which Hood constantly associates with the maternal? Žižek (2002) has made a strong argument for the link between trauma and love, claiming that trauma allows us to love that which is real for the subject through the subject's experience of lack in the symbolic order. I will challenge Žižek's interpretation by positing a relation to the real that can occur through the presence of the "imaginary father."

The concept of the imaginary father will be articulated through the work of the psychoanalytic theorist Julia Kristeva (1987). The imaginary father is the father of identification and idealization who, through the effect of the mirror, presents the subject with an image of the ego that allows a distance from the maternal container. Kristeva is at pains to emphasize the importance of this formation of the narcissistic ego for the emergence of the subject, as distinct from the hold of the primary maternal presence. And she takes issue with the Lacanian tendency to collapse the imaginary structure back into a form of autoeroticism that lacks any form of separation and freedom from the maternal. For Kristeva, the imaginary father is a figure (who can be either male or female) that is both like the mother and not like the mother, a figure that provides the mother's love but at a distance from the wrapping of the mother. The imaginary father is thus, in Kristeva's judgment, an important and necessary form of the third presence that comes between the maternal and the subject.

Yet, my challenge to Žižek's interpretation of trauma, an interpretation that emphasizes symbolic separation over imaginary bonds, is qualified. Kristeva herself, in some of her latest works (2000, 2002), has emphasized the importance of both the imaginary father and the oedipal father. Although the imaginary father is, in her view, necessary for the constitution of the subject, the oedipal father is as well. The oedipal father is the father of the symbolic law, and here

Kristeva agrees with the Lacanian emphasis (one echoed by Žižek) on the form of separation provided by the figure of law. The figure of law who says "no" is also a figure of love for the subject who, through the struggle with prohibition, allows the subject access to a world and the new and the exciting.

It will be my argument that Robert Hood's trauma is precipitated by an absence of both the imaginary father and the oedipal father, and that what he searches for in his journey north and what he longs for as he lies dying on the barrens is for a love that comes from both sides of the paternal. This is an important point to emphasize. I want to be clear that I am not arguing in this book that the uniqueness of northern love for masculine desire lies in the privileging of the imaginary father over the classic oedipal father. Rather, my intent is to articulate the missed possibilities that are inherent in imaginary love, and, moreover, that a law-like oedipal love that is shorn of these imaginary possibilities of love is problematic. You could say that the uniqueness of northern love is precisely the necessity for imaginary love to accompany oedipal love and that the uniqueness of Canadian masculinity in this regard is its ability to demonstrate that necessity.

⸻⸻⸻

As Sherrill Grace has emphasized, Robert Kroetsch is, along with Wiebe, a Canadian novelist who identifies himself with the North. The idea of Canada as a northern nation has been explored by Robert Kroetsch in an essay entitled "Why I Went Up North" (1995). Kroetsch's essay can be seen as inspiring his later imaginative explorations in the novel *The Man from the Creeks* (1998), which will be analyzed in detail in Section Two of this book. In "Why I Went Up North," Kroetsch tells us that when he was twenty years old he travelled to the North not to discover gold, but to write a novel. However, he soon discovers that the two searches are not so unrelated, that searching for gold and searching for words to write a story are, in fact, deeply connected. Kroetsch reflects on the poetic phrase "The men who moil for gold," indicating that to moil – to toil, to work hard – has a special signification in relation to the North, a signification that applies equally to the search for gold and the search for words.

To write is to step or stumble over the edge of the known into that category of desire that defines itself, always, just a hair's

breadth short of fulfillment. To write is, in some metaphorical
sense, to go North. To go North is, in some metaphorical sense,
to write. One goes North at the very point on the page where
the word is in the process of extending itself onto the blankness of the page. Whatever inscription might exist behind the
point of the pen, there can only be blankness ahead. (14)

What a trip to the North will teach the attentive observer is
the intricate relationship between word and space. Kroetsch explains
that it is the "uneasy relationship ... between the word one is writing
and the space that will contain the word and threaten it with erasure
that constitutes the Northward swerve." (15) As with Wiebe, there
is a sacrificial logic evident in Kroetsch's reflections. The movement
to the northern frontier represents an unravelling or shedding of the
self in the hopes of capturing a sense of freedom – here in Kroetsch's
reflections, the freedom of writing. Yet, Kroetsch also recognizes the
different forms of that quest – the difference between moving headlong
West, as the Americans seem to have done in keeping with their
European nation-state heritage, and the opportunity to move North
– when he tells us that "[t]he enduring impulse of European culture
is the impulse to go westward with latitude unwavering." (16) In
short, the rush westward refuses the movement northwards. Kroetsch
chooses to go North.

The movement North to capture once again the freedom of the
word can be viewed as a unique form of heroism. Kroetsch says that
"the trick is, often, to match a sense of destiny to a sense of the individual heroic act." (16) However, Kroetsch's understanding of a northern heroism does not comply with the usually understood form of
heroism often associated with the frontier, a heroism immortalized
for us in the American Western novel, where the hero conquers the
unknown. This is because a northern heroism is linked fundamentally
to the experience of silence. Kroetsch maintains that "[t]he North
was a silence that desired as much to be spoken as I desired to speak."
(16) He refers to an old Inuit man who had spent his entire life on
the tundra. For this Inuit man "there was hardly such a thing as
silence, only significant sound." (17) For Kroetsch, silence speaking
itself as significant sound becomes the inspiration for writing a novel
that is in homage to the North. This form of writing involves the
accurate representation of northern experience, an experience that
cannot be conceived of in the mode of conquering and controlling

the unknown. Kroetsch tells us that he conceived of a novel of the North "as the direct transport of experience onto a page." (17) That's why, back in 1948, he went up North: "I went up North to have the necessary experience; the novel would take care of itself." (17)

It wasn't until the 1990s that Kroetsch wrote a novel of the North that ties the search for words and story with the search for gold and the heroic act. *The Man from the Creeks* is a novel that liberally expands on the Robert Service poem "The Shooting of Dan McGrew." It follows the journey of Lou and her son Peek up the Alaskan coast and from Skagway to Chilkoot Pass, then down to Bennett City, and from there travelling down the Yukon River by boat to Dawson City and the Klondike Gold Rush. Lou and Peek are joined along the way by Ben, and then Gussie Meadows, and finally, in Dawson City, by Dan McGrew.

In Section Two of this book, I will explore in some detail the relationships that unfold between Lou, Peek, Ben, Gussie, and Dan in *The Man from the Creeks*. In particular, I will analyze the quest for gold as a quest for a heroic masculinity, one that, I believe, cannot be properly understood outside the context of the quest for intersubjective love. Tying the quest for gold and a heroic masculinity to intersubjective love may seem odd, given what Kroetsch has said in "Why I Went Up North" about moving into blankness and silence. In fact, Kroetsch has often been identified as one of the exemplary writers in the Canadian tradition who employs a kind of postmodern textuality, one that thrives on a movement past expectation into the nothingness of desire, a nothingness from which the freedom of writing draws its inspiration. I will argue in Section Two that the perspective emerging from *The Man from the Creeks* is one that can more properly be situated within a Hegelian understanding of intersubjective love.

There are three primary theoretical issues that I address in Section Two. As in Section One, these theoretical issues will be approached in the context of contemporary debates in psychoanalysis and social theory. My desire here will be to articulate the concept of intersubjective love by working through some significant theoretical debates around the Hegelian concepts of recognition, intersubjectivity, and the contract.

The first theoretical issue in Section Two concerns the concept of recognition. Kroetsch's novel begins with the emerging form of recognition between Lou and Ben as they travel north to the Klondike. Drawing on the work of the psychoanalytic feminist Jessica Benjamin

(1985), I will argue for an affirmative understanding of our identification with others and our dependency on their recognition. Within the context of mutuality, identification and recognition can produce a negation where the other emerges as an outside other who can provide the subject with ideals of change that are transformative. I want to argue for the connection of recognition and negativity and show how this connection is demonstrated in the ongoing relationship between Lou and Ben.

The second theoretical issue in Section Two concerns the concept of intersubjectivity. The concept of intersubjectivity is strongly tied to the workings of the dialectic. There are, however, different ways of interpreting the dialectic. Against the grain of Tiefensee's critique (1994, chapter 4) that Kroetsch's stories give us heroes whose dialectical struggles with otherness end up conquering and mastering otherness, I will argue that in *The Man from the Creeks* we are given heroes whose dialectical struggles with otherness do not conquer and master otherness, but reveal an intersubjective ground of love.

The debate over the dialectic will involve a turn to interpretations of Hegel. I will first look at Žižek's fascinating Lacanian defense of Hegel (1989, 1993), where he sees the move from external reflection to determinate reflection as the production of an alienated image grounded in pure negativity from which the subject reconciles himself with his lack. Thus, for Žižek, the Hegelian hero would not master otherness but, through the dialectical struggle, arrive at an absolute knowing of the non-mastery of otherness.

The problem, though, from the vantage point of this work, is that Žižek's Lacanian reading of Hegel demonstrates a considerable bias against the notion of intersubjectivity, believing that the bonds of intersubjectivity are tied to imaginary forms of misrecognition, especially a misrecognition of the subject's lack. I want to argue for the value of intersubjectivity in understanding the nature of Hegelian heroes. I will critique Žižek for ignoring the emergence in Hegel's *Logic* of an intersubjective structure. In contrast to Žižek, I will view the final movement of the "determinations of reflection" as being established through the concept of "ground" which allows for a relation between conflicting determinations that define subjects and a commonality that lies beyond singular perspectives. Peter Dews (1985) refers to this relation and this commonality as one of "love," a love that does not cancel the difference of subjects but retains difference through the dynamics of intersubjectivity.

On the basis of these reflections, I will argue that Hegelian heroes generally, and the particular heroes in *The Man from the Creek*, do not wish to close the gap between subjects through absolute knowing (Tiefensee and the critics of Hegel), nor are they seeking to work through negativity to the prime subjective awareness of lack (Žižek), but rather they seek out partnerships of love that form the ground for the freedom of their desire.

The third theoretical issue in Section Two concerns the concept of the contract. In attempting to make sense of the contract between Ben and Dan on the digging for gold and how that contrasts with the partnership established between Ben and Lou, I will turn once again to the work of Hegel and this time to his understanding of the contract in the *Philosophy of Right* (1981).

I will argue along with Hegel that, ideally, we can establish the contract on an intersubjective rather than individualistic ground. This begins with the understanding that the other is not a barrier to freedom but rather a realization of freedom. Despite some of the conservative readings of Hegel's notions of the family and community in the *Philosophy of Right,* I will maintain, along with Michael Theunissen (1991), that if we ground the contract in intersubjectivity we arrive at an expression of communal love that gives us access to a living good and a taste of universal life.

The fundamental movement in establishing an intersubjectively based contract is for the subjects in the contract to allow themselves to be exchangeable. This exchangeability of subjectivity occurs not through abstract identical wills, but through the movement from "mine-ness" to "own-ness" where a permanent tension is established between individuality and universality. My accomplishments are sublated in their immediacy, and thus shorn of their solipsism, by being presented in external form in the communal contract, where others see themselves through those accomplishments. Thus, I am, in my accomplishments, the other I am for others as they are the others they are for me.

My contention will be that Ben's understanding of the contract is through the structure of own-ness, and that understanding conflicts with Dan's which is that of mine-ness. This sets up the fateful showdown in the Malamute Saloon between Ben and Dan and the final episode in the "Shooting of Dan McGrew."

One of my main objectives in this book is to contribute to theoretical debates in psychoanalysis and social theory. My concept of northern love and my understanding of Canadian masculinity emerge first from the experience of the characters in the two novels by Wiebe and Kroetsch, and second from a theoretical interrogation of those experiences. In that sense, the theoretical articulations arise immanently, rather than externally, from the occasion of the experience of the characters. Yet, despite its base in the narrated experiences of the characters in the two novels, my articulations of the image and seeing, the relationship between the imaginary, symbolic and real, the understanding of trauma, the significance of recognition, inter-subjectivity and the contract, and the emerging concept of northern love in its relationship to Canadian masculinity, can be judged on their own merits as to the extent to which they contribute to those theoretical debates.

The organization of the book will take place according to both the unfolding of the narrated experiences of the principal characters in the two novels and the unfolding of the theoretical concepts that are engaged on the ground of that experience. Thus, Section One will be split into five chapters, and the five chapters are named according to the five theoretical issues spoken of above, namely, naming and seeing, master and slave, the imaginary, strange gender, and love and trauma. Section Two will be split into three chapters and also named according to the three theoretical issues referred to earlier, that is, recognition, intersubjectivity, and the contract.

Section

1

A STRANGE LOVE

1 NAMING AND SEEING

The first Franklin Expedition engages in a grand attempt to rename the entire North. There is a deep connection between English masculinity and the activity of naming. This activity of English naming is different from the activity of Tetsot'ine seeing. The English men of the first Franklin Expedition were never able to see the land they came to. We know that, in the end, they were quite literally reduced to blindness by cold and starvation. This blindness was there from the beginning and is made fully manifest later.

In this chapter, I would like to explore the conflict between naming and seeing by concentrating on the emerging relationship between Keskarrah, the Tetsot'ine shaman, and Robert Hood, an officer and sketcher on the Franklin Expedition, and on Hood's slowly learning to see the image that Keskarrah sees. Then I will draw on the theoretical work of Kaja Silverman (2000) to reflect on the difference between naming and seeing, or, in her terms, the difference between the word and the image.

Keskarrah, who greets the English as they arrive, laughs when he encounters John Franklin, the leader of the English Expedition, who explains to him that the English had come here for their benefit. In their discovery excursion to the North the English did not take notice of the snowshoes given to them and were not aware of the Tetsot'ine who supported them. The English were hell-bent on travelling North to "discover" a passage through the northern ice. Keskarrah responds incredulously: "The lake and river ice thundered cold at them the whole year they were carried to us.... Again and again. How much more did These English have to be told?" (Wiebe 1994, 15) For Keskarrah, any telling of this sort comes in the form of seeing; the English men were not able to tell the danger because they could not see the signs of danger in front of them. They were too busy in their quest to name the land. In Keskarrah's view, the image comes before speaking and the word.

It seems that the English men "had heard only their own telling, as told to themselves." (15) This speaks to a particular form of psychic closure on the part of the English sailors, an inability to open a space of care for the Being of things to reveal themselves in image and story. Even though Keskarrah has heard stories of the English, now that they have arrived, they are 'impossible to forget." (17) Before, the Tetsot'ine only needed to think of their people, their land, and their life as it had been for a long time. Now "a fireball smashed through the sky: crash! – here, are Whites!" (17) With the Whites, "the world is always on fire with something else." (17) When the Whites arrived at the edge of the water the paddlers in the canoe made "a great, driving sound." (17) Their enormous canoe "rams ashore." (18) The canoes stand "erect, motionless." (19) We witness here a peculiar presence of the English phallus, attempting to assert its power, covering over its own lack.

When Franklin, the leader of the English Expedition, steps ashore, Birdseye, the wife of Keskarrah, says to her husband: "Look." (18) Keskarrah looks carefully, but does not speak. Greenstockings, his daughter, expects her father to say something, because he "understands much." (19) Keskarrah, however, says nothing. Even at the council circle that has been convened with the White leader, Keskarrah says nothing, allowing Big Foot to speak, who the Whites think is the Tetsot'ine "chief."

Instead of speaking, Keskarrah begins to draw. He draws "a very small picture of the land." (19) And he says, "if These English are to know anything, you will have to name it." (19) Keskarrah then proceeds to give precise names to the possible river routes the English can take to move north. Keskarrah's recourse to drawing rather than speaking means that, for the Tetsot'ine, vision is given priority.

This emphasis on vision is repeated when Keskarrah, Birdseye, and Greenstockings first meet Robert Hood, an officer and sketcher on the Expedition. Keskarrah asks Birdseye: "What is it you see?" Birdseye sees the "younger one ... the last, the thin one." (20) He is "a slender, wind-broken tree, walking." (20) He is "nothing ... only bone." (21) Keskarrah thinks that may just be his skin, which looks sodden. Birdseye replies that it isn't just the skin, it's the bones: "like the Snowman." (21) If he is the Snowman then surely bad weather follows. Who is the Snowman, what is his story? His is "a story of a stranger, of danger, coming and going." (21)

Greenstockings is fascinated by the thin skin of Hood. Later, "she will discover that his skin is not at all hard, and that his hair ... is crinkled light brown, not black and hard and straight." (21) At that moment, a new connection is asserted, the connection between seeing and touching. Greenstockings will "pull her hand all around his head, as if with her fingers in his he could draw his face into a circle." (21) She understands "that he is making a picture of his name with her hand around his face, *hood*." (22) This is all very strange to her. She wonders what her mother has seen and what her father has touched, "when if ever, it has been possible for his fingers to find such skin under them." (22) To see and touch such difference. And on the basis of her seeing and her touching of this strange creature, she will try to say his name, Hood: "she will try to shape her lips into a puckered, protruding 'O' like his and puff air at him, 'ooo...ooo....'" (22) Even though Hood tries, "he will never be able to say her name at all, not even the middle of it as she can his." (22)

The rest of the Whites will not even try to say her Tetsot'ine name. This is because they do not have the ability to name something that has been grounded in the experience of seeing and touching. The English try to "name every lake and river with whatever sound slips from their mouths." (22) Yet, without the long-standing material experience of the land gained through seeing and touching this is difficult: "it is truly difficult for a few men who glance at it once to name an entire country." (22)

This attitude of the English extends to "the racket and unending busyness of guns." (23) It seems that the lure of "guns and powder" has captured the Tetsot'ine men as well. Keskarrah hates the guns, they scream, "Listen: I'M HERE!" (23) This sound of guns is analogous to the activity of English naming, a presence that announces itself so insistently, in such a demanding way, so different from a quiet, patient response. The English shoot at the deer in the river indiscriminately "instead of floating in tiny canoes on the silent water and spearing fast." (23)

For the Tetsot'ine "every place already was its true and exact name." (24) Birdseye and Keskarrah "knew the land, each name a story complete in their heads." (24) The names which are stories are tied to seeing. Keskarrah could see. He could see "in the shape and turn of an eddy, the broken brush at the last edge of the trees, the rocks of every place he waited for caribou." (24) And Birdseye has walked everywhere, demonstrating that there is an intimate connection between seeing and walking. The People see and walk and then name and tell stories, "the way any Tetsot'ine must if they would live the life of this land." (24)

Keskarrah draws the places he knows "through his fingers from behind his eyes onto the ground, which is where all land already lies fully and complete, though hidden." (24) Or he will draw on birchbark using dead embers from the fire, "because the seeds and roots of trees are always in the land, and the seed and root of fire live eternally within trees. Names are waiting to be breathed out again, quietly, into the air." (25) Names come from the body and the earth. Keskarrah explains that "just making a sound can mean... nothing." Rather, "it is for us to look. Perhaps we will recognize how everything alive is already within everything else." (25)

———————

Kaja Silverman, in *World Spectators*, can help us make sense of the priority given to seeing by the Tetsot'ine. In this work, Silverman extends her proposal, initiated in earlier works, that the visual image has priority over other forms of representation.

Silverman claims that appearance is not primarily a linguistic disclosure, but "insistently visual." (3) Yet, vision has been denigrated in the Western tradition, a tradition that grounds the English masculinity of the Expedition and their activity of naming. Silverman begins to articulate a different perspective by turning to Lacan, who argues that the source of production for visual forms is a mysterious nonentity, *das Ding*, the "impossible nonobject of desire." (15) This is itself a departure from Freud: we are not oriented then toward an original love object; rather, the object "becomes an object only in its absence" through "retroactive symbolization." (16)

Silverman believes that this attempt to understand the activity whereby things appear in vision is aided by a turn to Heidegger. To care and release a creature into its Being we need to make sense of it in its visual diversity. Heidegger's problem, though, according to Silverman, is that he articulates Being in non-psychic terms. Yet, while Lacan emphasizes the psyche, the problem is that his emphasis on a psychic void overlooks the movement toward the world through care. Maybe bringing Heidegger and Lacan together will help.

Silverman claims that the disclosure of objects requires the experience of loss. This experience of loss gives rise to a desire to symbolize what we have lost. Lacan's perspective is that the lost object is a non object, *das Ding*. This means that the orientation is to the loss of Being, not to the loss of the original love object. For Silverman, this emphasis on loss has an important consequence: "[It] opens the way toward something many of us have long dreamed of: an a-oedipal or even anti-oedipal psychoanalysis." (40)

Yet, according to Silverman, Lacan is not interested in going in that direction; for Lacan, the loss of Being must be repeated through castration in the Oedipus complex. Silverman agrees that the experience of loss must be repeated, because the non-object cannot connect us to the world of things. This connection is performed by the representatives of the non-object which we love when we lose Being. She claims that we lose then love, not love then lose. If the latter prevailed, then the only path to desire would be to recoup our first loves.

There is a problem here, though. Silverman has already indicated dissatisfaction with Lacan's account of the original void: nothing cannot connect us to something. The turn to Heidegger has convinced her that, rather than there being an original void, there is an original mode of care which directs desire toward the world of things. This mode of care is intimately connected to the maternal, the original love of the mother. And if care is maternal, our return to origins is a return to the original love of the mother which connects us to the world. Perhaps we do not lose then love, but love and lose at the same time, where love and loss are inseparable; we cannot understand one without the other.

These considerations will be important as we proceed, because we will see later that both Hood and Greenstockings experience a return to origins. What is the nature of this return and how is it connected to the relationship between seeing and naming, and seeing and touching? And how is this return connected to the experience of love and loss?

Silverman's argument concerning the centrality of the visual image begins by showing how Lacan transforms the sign from the Sausserian heritage. For Lacan, perceptual signifiers precede verbal signifiers, looking precedes speaking, and the image precedes the word. Moreover, it is only in perceptual signifiers that things become affectively present. This occurs in the transference which begins linguistically – we address our words to the other and they return to us as signifiers. Yet, according to Silverman, the transference is a general social event, a theatrical event. Those who hear the actor's speech are not listeners, but spectators. Through speech they see something. And thus saying becomes showing, a visual affirmation.

Silverman grounds the argument for the libidinal production of images in Freud. It is in the displacement of kinship that libidinal speech becomes possible. This is not an abstract process. We speak libidinally by producing images, not abstract notations. Silverman claims that "[t]he basic drive in the human subject is the urge to see more than what has been seen before." (78) The psyche is therefore established as an optical device with the analogy drawn between psyche and camera. This analogy goes back to Freud in *The Interpretation of Dreams*. For Freud, perceptual stimulus only becomes conscious when it coalesces with a memory from the unconscious. These memories have a force of attraction in their struggle to achieve perceptual form.

Silverman believes that this perspective of Freud, articulated in his early work, leads to a unique understanding of the pleasure principle, different from the one usually attributed to Freud. The pleasure principle is not oriented toward reducing excitation, but increasing it. There are two sources of stimulation, one from the external world, and the other from unconscious memory. As they coalesce, there is not a discharge of excitation, but a displacement from memory to external perception. In fact, there is a pleasure in not being satisfied, in giving oneself over to displacement. The pleasure principle is thus "the enabling force behind a particular kind of looking." (92) According to Silverman, Freud's position points to numerous scopic possibilities, which are, in effect, possibilities of showing. Here, there is pleasure in reviving an earlier memory by linking it to a new external perception in the present.

This pleasure is grounded in the thing-presentation and not the word-presentation. The linguistic signifier, or word-presentation, is closed to affective transfers. On the other hand, the perceptual signifier, or thing-presentation, is open to affective transfers. The word-presentation is linked to the preconscious-conscious system. The preconscious binds the unconscious memory by linking it to a linguistic signifier. This inhibits the transfer of affective energy and curtails the pathways where energy might go. The thing-presentation is open to libidinal transfer. In Silverman's reading of Freud, the unconscious forms around an ideational representation that is primarily repressed. The force of the drive then occurs with the force of this primary repression. The primarily repressed term then places a second term in its place. And the second prevents the first from entering the preconscious. For Silverman, the primarily repressed thing-presentation realizes itself by allowing another thing-presentation to take its place. This generates a constant displacement that keeps desire moving. It also involves an anti-cathexis. The preconscious anti-cathexis attempts to reduce excitation by connecting thing-presentation to word-presentation. On the other hand, the unconscious anti-cathexis creates excitation by facilitating the transfer of energy from original to secondary thing-presentation.

Silverman's reflections help us to make better sense of the conflict between Tetsot'ine seeing and English naming. Keskarrah's emphasis on seeing the land is one that draws on unconscious desire in the ability to return to the source of all representation, the non-object of desire. And the non-object, if grounded in the care of the maternal, can reveal the things of the world in a visual diversity of forms. To see is also to love, to see from the standpoint of love. In contrast, English naming remains fixed in the conscious ego, which attempts to master the world of things. Thus, English naming removes itself from a movement back to the non-object of desire and a movement back to the ground of maternal care. The result for the English word that names is a narrowing of affect to the controlling stance of the ego and an inability to see the things of the world in their visual diversity. It also represents an inability to love and experience love.

2 MASTER AND SLAVE

The English men of the Franklin Expedition consider themselves masters of all the people they encounter in the New World, especially the Aboriginal men and women, considering them for the most part as slaves. This is particularly true of George Back, an officer on the Expedition, who treats both the men and women of the Tetsot'ine with disgust. In this chapter, both Back's understanding of the master-slave dynamic and Greenstockings' response to that understanding will be articulated. Greenstockings is angry. She is angry at the slave-like position that women in particular occupy, especially in the imagination of the English, and for Back in particular. I will then move on to theoretically engage the Hegelian master-slave dialectic by working through Judith Butler's reading of that dialectic. Through this theoretical and conceptual exploration, I will argue that the unfolding of northern love involves an articulation of the productive position of the slave in the unfolding of desire.

Greenstockings wants to know what the other young man's name means, the one who "does not seem to know how to draw his name in the air" and "will do almost everything else with [her hand] except that." (27) His name is Back, and Greenstockings thinks it fits: "his short back is much stronger than slender Hood's." (27) He is able to lift Greenstockings "easily over his curly head" such that "she is forced to know, as with every man she has ever met, the power of his name: 'George Back!'" (28)

Thinking of Back, Greenstockings is led to think of "everyman." She thinks of those who are powerful and force their presence, their name, upon her. She knows where the English men keep their names, which for her is inherently dangerous. She also knows where her mother keeps her name, which for her is not dangerous. In what ways does Hood participate in these dangerous manly characteristics mentioned by Greenstockings? Or alternatively, in what ways does he deviate from them, such that he no longer is "everyman"? In what way does Hood keep a name where his mother keeps hers?

As Back attempts to overpower her "she feels him shift hard between her thighs like every man always has, hard bone." (28) Everyman announces his name through a hard bone. Greenstockings remembers how Back's hands grappled for her. Back's grappling hands are contrasted with the hands of her mother, Birdseye: "Once those hands fondled Greenstockings until she cried in ecstasy, cried in ways the four men who have already fought and nearly killed themselves over her cannot find anywhere in the brief duration of their manly imaginations." (29) All the men who fight over her cannot bring her the pleasure that comes from her mother's touch, the maternal touch, the ground of care.

We soon discover that Hood will fight over Greenstockings, in a classic duel with Back. Does this mean that Hood is just like Everyman? Earlier Greenstockings had noticed the peculiarity or strangeness of Hood's hands in drawing his name with her hand on his skin. In that instant, Hood's name and hands and skin are different from "everyman." Greenstockings often feels that "men's hands are fit only to clutch knives, to claw at clubs and lances, to strip hide or flesh from dead bones, to knot into fists, perhaps – now – to grope and jerk at triggers." (29) To clutch and strip and knot and grope and jerk – that is what defines Everyman's hands for Greenstockings.

Greenstockings' Tetsot'ine husband, Broadface, has had his left hand severely mangled from a gun misfiring. Greenstockings asks:

What can a person fondle with such a hand? Broadface is strong enough to carry a grizzly, but a woman does not need such force to be entered. Greenstockings thinks that all the men, including the Tetsot'ine men, treat their women like the Whites treat the land: forceful entry.

According to Greenstockings' account, Back, who is also a sketcher on the Expedition, "can draw his own short back in one line so fast you can see it exactly, the way it bends, and then he curls the bottom end of it up, pointing down at himself, he's so proud, hooked up as he draws it almost as long!" (30) The strong back of Back is inseparable from his hard bone, inseparable from the enduring image of his backbone. The Tetsot'ine women with Greenstockings respond in shouts of laughter to her description of Back. They can see that he has backbone. Back tries to "tower" with his tall hat, acting "imperiously" by pointing everywhere, ordering work from those he considers his slaves. The Tetsot'ine women laugh at Back and mock him. They chant, "Back, back, bone of a back!" (31)

One of the women, Angelique, who has married a mixed-blood, and knows of the English, comments that "maybe the thin young one could draw his name out of his bone too." (31) She says that in English his name can mean "cap." To which another responds that Hood must be able to draw his name from his bone, because "every man has a cap on his bone!" (31) And they all laugh again, laughing "at the same dangly, miserable, hard thing about men." (31) Angelique interrupts their laughter by saying that "sometimes Whites don't have any cap there ... because they think they'll be stronger then, they cut that cap off." (31)

Greenstockings and the other Tetsot'ine women seem to be commenting on a particular imaginary illusion of the English men they have encountered, men who think they can become stronger through the power of the cut. It is a general tenet of Lacanian theory that the oedipal cut is necessary for the experience of lack, lack constituting the privileged entry into the social and representing a movement away from the illusions of the imaginary. Is the cut, though, needed to experience loss? Is there the necessity of the cut for there to be a retroactive symbolization of an originary loss, based in the non-object of desire? It seems that this is what the English men believe, what they believe about the phallus: cutting the phallus makes a man stronger.

However, the Tetsot'ine women understand "the simple and continually unfathomable burden women must carry – all men. For the strangers clearly are men." (32) The women understand "the inescapable power and fear – sometimes joy, often brutality, even terror – that men forever carry about them like their cocks, limp or rigid, hanging somehow gently, possibly tender or abruptly lethal ... thrust ... jerk ... grab, ram, pound into them." (32) Yet, at the same time, Greenstockings' skin remembers how Back and Hood were so different from each other, as well as different form Broadface. This means that Hood demonstrates a different form of masculinity from the other men, one that does not originate from the cut.

We need to be reminded that Greenstockings' critique of everyman includes a critique of the Tetsot'ine men. She extends that critique in a conversation with her mother, Birdseye. Birdseye says to Greenstockings that Thick English (Franklin) wants the best Tetsot'ine hunters to kill animals for his men. And that Bigfoot, one of the Tetsot'ine leaders, says they will do this. Yet, Greenstockings wonders how Bigfoot can do this; he is not their boss – they have no boss or chief. Moreover, Greenstockings can't figure out why the men would do it. Perhaps the men really do want to hunt for the Whites? Maybe the men have been seduced by the Whites and their guns? And suddenly Greenstockings "feels a woman's contempt for this illogical acquiescence, this feeble agreement of all accepting what a stranger wants of them." (34)

Birdseye responds by saying that the Whites have so many things that the men want. Bigfoot will get "another shiny medal" (35) which he seems to prize dearly. The English will give the hunters "more tea ... then whisky ... more nets for fishing and more guns and more bullets and powder." (35) Greenstockings replies: "Things piled up! Is that what our men think should happen?" (35) Theirs is a society on the move, light, walking. How are they supposed to carry these things, all these heavy things? And it is primarily the burden of women to carry and cook. Where are the English women? Greenstockings thinks that the Tetsot'ine women now become slaves for the English men. She links this form of slavery to the acquiescence of the Tetsot'ine men. She says, "Yes! All our mighty men agree ... and they pile those things on us to carry.... Let them freeze stiff as cocks in their cloth!" (36)

Birdseye thinks Greenstockings' words "are as strange in the mouth, or the ears, of a woman as anything These English have dragged into their country." (36) She believes that "anger is always dangerous." (37) Yet, as her mother, Birdseye understands that

Greenstockings' strange angry words are in response to a strange feeling her daughter has. She asks: "What is it? What have you felt?" (37) Birdseye will not let Greenstockings avoid confronting this feeling, this transfer of affect that comes from the other. Birdseye continues with her motherly questions: "What have you felt... When you feel all over that head, those Snow Man arms and hands feeling you?" Is it that Greenstockings' strange anger at her own Tetsot'ine men is associated with her strange desire for Hood, a man who is, according to the English standards, a strange man?

Perhaps the angry voice of Greenstockings can be understood through the ambivalent workings of the master-slave dialectic. When we first hear the English voice, in particular the voice of George Back, we hear an articulation of the master-slave relationship, a relationship that quickly unravels. Back acknowledges that "the Indians must work for us if our expedition is not to prove impossible." (46) And, given this dependency, he also acknowledges the usefulness of Franklin's strategy of treating the Tetsot'ine "with the distant gravity of King George III himself." (46) At the same time, Back is annoyed and troubled by this acceptance of the power and dignity of the Tetsot'ine: "if we permit and help enact such pretentious charades for too long, I am confident disaster will strike." (47) Thus, Back thinks disaster will come if they (the English) acknowledge their dependency on the Tetsot'ine at the level of symbolic dignity, a recognition of equal status.

When Back considers the Tetsot'ine male he is ambivalent: he marvels at "his stitched-together retinue of leather and fur and nakedness.... [and] strong handsome limbs." But he also sees a "wild people" who seem not to "know what work is." (47) And despite seeing the need to enter into an agreement with the Tetsot'ine that accords them symbolic dignity, Back says that "the native must obey us if we are to succeed." (47) The Tetsot'ine male must obey the English male even though the English male is dependent on the Tetsot'ine male. Back says: "they must find and kill enough deer to feed us and all our labouring men." (47)

We have in Back's commentary an expression of the master-slave relationship. If we are to believe Judith Butler, in her commentary on the master-slave relationship in Hegel, the slave's encounter with autonomy in relation to the master comes through the experience of fear. (1997: 39–41) This fear relates to the subject's loss of control through labour, a loss that speaks to a profound feeling of transience. This reverses things somewhat, according to Butler. It would seem, at first glance, that the master is the one who is able to experience the transience of life because it is the master who consumes everything that the slave produces, leaving nothing behind, nothing of permanence, and that the slave is the one who experiences permanency because of the creating of permanent things. For the master, the transitory status of the object is related to the transitory state of desire, whereas for the slave the permanence of object-filled labour leads to the permanence and fixity of desire. Yet, now we see that the relationship is quite different. According to Butler, the slave experiences a unique form of loss in relation to the object, due to the fact that he is constantly losing the object, giving the object up to the master to be consumed. Although the slave gives form to objects through labour, and thus creates a kind of permanence, that permanence does not last, because the object is quickly gone, consumed.

In the case of the Tetsot'ine male hunters, hunting for them is a production that is oriented around loss. The Tetsot'ine men realize that what they hunt will be taken by the English men. However, they are not forced into this, but do so willingly, as a fundamental mode of being of their culture and of their desire, to give up the object to the other. This is because the experience of loss is one that marks their productive practice whether the English are there or not. They gain, they lose, understanding that for small bands thriving in the North, gain is never permanent. If they trade, they trade for what they need at the moment.

On the basis of Butler's analysis, we can identify an important characteristic in the Tetsot'ine male hunter's experience of loss. If the male hunter places his signature on the hunted object, and we know that that object is sacrificed, then the male hunter shows himself to be a being marked by sacrifice. His signature is a form of self-erasure, a kind of vanishing of his subjectivity. The male hunter demonstrates that what is irreducibly his own is his own vanishing, and that this vanishing occurs through the presence of an other, an other for which he provides in the mode of care.

It is important to note here the presence of a sacrificial logic, for that will constitute a fundamental feature of desire in the unfolding of this story. If sacrifice is the logic of the Tetsot'ine male hunter, what happens when he is seduced by the English male logic of the commodity? For the English man, in his position as master, faces an impasse, not only because of his unacknowledged dependency on the Tetsot'ine male, but also, and probably more importantly, because his consumption is marked by a lack of consciousness of loss – the English master seeks to accumulate property, to build up, to create heaviness, permanence. If the Tetsot'ine male desires what the English male has, then he in effect gives up his position as one who achieves freedom through vanishing, through the sacrifice of self. This is what Greenstockings is disgusted with as she witnesses the transformation of desire in her people's men.

Moreover, are not the turns and twists of the master-slave relationship related to the relationship between seeing and naming, in Silverman's terminology, between word-presentation and thing-presentation? Although the name or word of the English conceives of itself as independent of the bodily and earthly thing, the Tetsot'ine attachment to seeing the thing belies that. It turns out that the seeing of the Tetsot'ine, especially the dream-seeing of Keskarrah, is what guides the English through the North, except when the English dismiss that dream-seeing, much to their peril, and rely on their name-based technology. Indeed, there is a solidarity between the stasis of the English name or word and the stasis of English technology, in that neither is open to affective transfers, and thus to the experience of loss, an experience only possible through a kind of dream-seeing.

Keskarrah is a dream-seer, and it is interesting to see Back contrasting the Tetsot'ine shaman's masculinity with that of the masculinity of Franklin, the commander of the Expedition. Back refers to Keskarrah as a "hesitating old man" (48), while he admires Franklin for his planned decisiveness as a commander. To Back, Keskarrah seems confused about the route that the English should take, seems confused about a return river. The Tetsot'ine fear what they called the "Everlasting Ice", which for them demands an awareness of how to return. However, Back tells the Tetsot'ine that "we have no intention of returning again this way." (48) Although English planning does not fear the Arctic, Back registers this fear in speaking of the voyageur's lack of experience on an "ice-filled ocean." (49)

Hood expresses to Back his concern for the Tetsot'ine, given that the English have hired the best hunters in the Tetsot'ine band. He wonders "who will feed all their families this winter." (49) Hood conveys to Back that this assistance goes beyond the hunters to the Tetsot'ine women, who will have to help the three voyageur women skin and cut and dry the meat. These concerns of Hood irk Back, who finds annoying Hood's speaking in "moral imperatives," what he refers to as "the dry echo of a small clergyman." (50) This is a clear reference to Hood's father, who is an Anglican priest. We will have an opportunity later to consider the extent to which Hood's voice appropriates the voice of his preacher-father.

In response to Hood's concerns, Back simply states the obvious: the Tetsot'ine leader, Bigfoot, has committed them. Is Bigfoot their leader? Remember Greenstockings saying that Bigfoot has no right to commit her people because he is not the leader, even if the English think so. As well, Greenstockings recognizes the hardship this will bring to the Tetsot'ine women. Hood intuits the voice of Greenstockings, a voice already aberrant to the Tetsot'ine, when he asks, concerning Bigfoot: "A leader does not consider the disadvantages for his people?" (50)

What constitutes leadership anyway? Hood compares Bigfoot to Napoleon, who also betrayed his people. Back finds the comparison ludicrous: "this greasy primitive." (50) This echoes his earlier dismissal of Franklin's attempt to create an analogy between the Tetsot'ine conflict with the northern Inuit and the conflicts of Europe: "What can the inhabitants of such a desolate land understand concerning political and national philosophies of Empire? To compare their elementary hostilities to England's conflict with Napoleon ... is ludicrous." (44) To Back, the Inuit have "no discernible social organization" and are "wandering about at random." (44)

However, more is at stake in the attempt by Hood to draw in the figure of Napoleon. He refers sarcastically to Napoleon as "the short Great Emperor." (50) Back clearly sees Hood's slight against him. He responds: "Hood can only resort to the elementary accident of his own length. Though I outweigh him by two stone and can easily outwalk him twice in a day." Back seems to be saying: I may not be long, but I am heavy and strong.

For Hood, though, Back is aligned with Bigfoot in thinking in terms of power and strategic advantage while disregarding the overall welfare of the people. In this he is in agreement with Greenstockings, who also slides from a negative appraisal of Back to a negative appraisal of Bigfoot – to her, that is what men do, there is nothing can you do about it.

The twists and turns of the English-Tetsot'ine/master-slave scenario are played out in a similar vein in the relationship between the English sailors and the Canadian voyageurs. This is especially true in the mutiny of the Canadians. We are told that "all their working lives these men have portaged 180-pound packs, and four of them can carry the 600-pound canoe over any rocky defile without betraying the slightest weariness." (51) The Canadian men exhibit a particular form of "male pride." (51) This is manifested in them being able to "wrestle or dance around their fires even after fourteen hours of indescribable labour." (51)

Back, a British naval officer, registers a fascination with the masculine character of the voyageur men who serve the British. He says that their songs "bespeak a certain courageous humanity." (51) Despite this fascination, Back reports that if the Canadian men are in mutiny, they must be dealt with swiftly. Back is annoyed at Hood for not instantly reacting as a British officer should. Hood is simply "standing there with nothing but pencil and paper in hand." (51) Hood has pencil and paper instead of a loaded gun.

The Canadian voyageurs have had little to eat for seven days and they are refusing to work any more that day until they are provided with fresh meat. Again, despite his admiration for particular masculine features of their character, Back here claims that the "weathercock minds of Canadians are stirred to reflection only by their bellies." (52) The Canadian men – who are half-breeds, French and native – may be strong and courageous but they cannot reflect like the British.

Franklin responds to their mutiny by reminding the Canadian men of their "contracted duty" and that he will treat them like English sailors and punish them if they do not obey. Hood finally walks up, in Back's words, "very calmly, still holding his futile pencil." (53) And not his gun loaded. The ironic thing here is that Back realizes that the Canadian men could easily overtake the three officers with loaded pistols – Back, Franklin, and Richardson (Hood is useless with his pencil). As the voyageurs advance, Back, Franklin, and Richardson raise their pistols. Although the two biggest voyageurs and the Mohawk continue to advance, sixteen in their group have stopped. Back is amazed: they could crush us. But, as he says, "no Canadian can outface British character." (54) The character of the Canadian men is strong and courageous, but the steely resolve of the British officer with his drawn pistol overmatches their brute strength. The mutiny is over, and the Canadian men are to be docked three full days' pay.

Back's characterizations of the Tetsot'ine men and the Canadian men are reproduced, in slightly different form, by his commander, Sir John Franklin. To Franklin, the Hudson's Bay traders who had traded with the Tetsot'ine were "very lax in establishing any sense of duty required by a work contract." (58) In fact, the hunters "lacked almost completely the discipline necessary for efficient service to the Expedition." (59)

These comments indicate the extent to which the traditional Tetsot'ine male hunter throws a wrench in the master-slave drama. The Canadian men seem to be more open to a commonly understood expression of the master-slave drama. The Canadian men can work efficiently. And they can produce in such a way that the English can consume. Franklin's assessment is that the Tetsot'ine men do not seem to be able to produce like the Canadian men do. For Franklin, "only an extended and very firm experience of English order would achieve that [the sense of duty] – as it had for the voyageurs." (59) Only this sense of duty will allow the Tetsot'ine men to produce for the English. This intensifies the production-loss bond mentioned earlier. The very production of the Tetsot'ine male hunters is marked by a lack that the English men find troubling.

Dr. Richardson agrees with Franklin's analysis. Richardson is a man who exhibits a "trained Scottish thoroughness." (59) His note-books are "full of numbers ... including decimal points." (59) He says to Franklin, "we will never control any Indians, not in this wild country, until we teach them the absolute, practical necessity of money." (59) Franklin responds: "They hardly seem to require it; since they trade for what they need." (59) Richardson believes this is the "fundamental problem in the economic development of primitives. If they understood money, they would work harder to get more of it, in order to buy what they want." (59). To Franklin's comment that the Tetsot'ine do not seem to want that much, Richardson responds, "they must want more than they need. That is civilization." (59)

Richardson, thinking the English to be the master, believes that the master's position is one that allows him to freely desire. He believes that the use of money and technology will bring a freeing up of want into insatiable desire, the mark of civilization. Yet, the use of money, as we know from Marx, can quickly lead not to free desire, but to a want of money, and a stasis of character and culture that requires the order and discipline to acquire more money. So a reversal is in place: what looked like the master's open desire and the slave's stasis turns into the master's stasis and the slave's open desire. For it is the Tetsot'ine who, in not wanting to take on the order and discipline of duty required for a money economy, are able to continually experience the ground of loss that opens them to desire. But have they really rejected this offer? Greenstockings' assessment is that the Tetsot'ine men seem to be eagerly taking up the project of the master: give me guns, give me gold chains, give me commodities, give me property.

3 THE IMAGINARY

We begin this chapter with an exploration of Tetsot'ine mourning and the anxiety that their particular encounter with loss creates for the English explorers. The position of mourning is particularly acute for Greenstockings, who transfers the experience of mourning the lost hunters to her own particular struggle in mourning the loss of maternal love. I will make sense of this experience of the loss of maternal love by engaging a theoretical debate between Slavoj Žižek and Judith Butler on the status of the imaginary in relation to the symbolic and the real. In particular, I will make use of Butler's critique of Žižek and other Lacanians to highlight the productive nature of the imaginary in its relation to lost possibilities of love.

⇥•⇤

The English associate the Tetsot'ine with lack. This is made especially evident when the English witness a Tetsot'ine mourning ritual and the encounter the Tetsot'ine have with loss. As they look to the shores of Winter Lake, to the slim, twisted trees, the English continue to be suspicious of the old man Keskarrah and his prediction that they will soon come upon an esker of large trees to build shelter for the winter. However, just as they discuss these reservations, the Tetsot'ine are gone, having forged ahead to a distant island. The English do not see them, but hear the sound, "a sound they could not order, a tintin-nabulation of insanities." (61) The Tetsot'ine are on an island and "they were jumping wildly about ... shrieking." (61)

The English cannot order the sound, and Hood cannot order his sketch. He cannot capture "a coherent quadrant of the world through which he was being carried." (61) The vistas ahead of him are widening and Hood feels himself "tugged towards a periphery in the corner of his eye that, when he yielded, was still never there." (62) This is a strange drawing experience for Hood, one where "he felt his body slowly tighten, twist; as if it were forming into a gradual spiral that might turn his head off at the neck." (62) Just "[l]ike one of those pathetic little trees." (62) Hood experiences an affective transfer to the trees on the shore of the lake. Although he discovers "that perfect sphere of unbordered sameness" so often associated with northern tundra, at that very moment of this discovery, he also understands "that the continuous world was, nevertheless, not at all or anywhere ever the same." (62) We have already referred (in chapter 1) to the confusion of boundaries that is experienced in the Canadian North because of the distinctive confluence of land, river, lake, and ocean. The confusion of boundaries leads to a confusion of aware-ness. And the confusion of [boundaries?] makes for a unique mode of desire in the drawing experience, one that lacks the dependable frame to capture an image. Hood experiences disorientation, a loss of control, one that he is not used to.

Ahead on the island, the Tetsot'ine are experiencing loss as well. From one loss to another. Two Tetsot'ine hunters have been killed and the distant lake has not yet given them back. The English now witness what they call "Indian grief." (63) The English officers "could not in a lifetime have imagined such grief." (63) The Tetsot'ine

> were overwhelmed with bellows and weeping and screams ...
> with lodgepoles being broken and skins ripped, kettles crushed,
> axes splintered, dogs throats being slit, and everything, any
> thing or animal that came to hand, smashed and torn and
> bleeding, being flung everywhere into the lake. The small island
> blazed with the necessity of destruction. The Yellowknives

were attacking their canoes, breaking the very guns with which they were to hunt. (63)

Why are the Tetsot'ine making themselves poor? Judith Butler, in *The Psychic Life of Power* (23–25) follows Freud's analysis and speaks of the difference between a mourning of the lost object and a melancholia that signals uncompleted grief. For Butler, mourning involves a longing to grieve, not just the loss of the object which has died, but, through a grieving of the lost object, a grieving of the lost possibilities of love, those objects one was never able to love. This is an experience of the loss of the loss, an awareness through grieving of the always already lost object. Melancholia, on the other hand, marks an inability to grieve, an inability to grieve not only the loss of the object but also the lost possibilities of love. Melancholia represents an attachment, an attachment to the attachment that is broken or lost, a stubborn attachment.

The Tetsot'ine in their grief have attempted to destroy their possessions. They destroy the order and security that possessions symbolically bring to the psyche. They destroy the symbolic law of society that depends for its reproduction on acquiring possessions. The symbolic law is grounded in the power of the father, where the father's word considers itself master to the screaming voices of the Tetsot'ine. We could also say that the English horror at the Tetsot'ine mourning speaks to a melancholic mood, an attachment to the father's word as the symbolic law of society, an attachment to the master's discourse that forecloses the route back through dispossession and screaming to the lost possibilities of love.

The attachment the English have to the word of the father is demonstrated when, after leaving the Tetsot'ine to continue their grief, they paddle on and at the end of Winter Lake they find Keskarrah's forest, exactly where the old man had promised it would be. The place was ideal: "stream water, many large trees, the shelter of the esker against the northern winds and its dry, coarse sand for a foundation ... [and] excellent white clay ... for chinking between house logs." (67) The contrast here is stark. The Tetsot'ine experience the loss of loss, while the English begin to build a winter settlement and give thanks to the father as Franklin, their commander, performs Sunday services. This invocation of the father's word reinstitutes a symbolic order of the father, a control and permanence for the English in the face of the troubling sense of loss that they witnessed in the Tetsot'ine. Instead of the screams and wailing dance, the English have the words carefully prescribed by the Anglican *Book of Common Prayer*. The anxiety experienced by the English in the face of Tetsot'ine mourning indicates an inability to mourn, and the attempt to reinstitute a particular form of melancholy, one that, through a stubborn attachment, sets up the word of the father in place of the lost object and the lost possibilities of love.

This inability to mourn the lost object is a distinctive feature of English masculinity. In fact, it is an enduring feature of masculinity of not only the English men, but also the Tetsot'ine men.

Greenstockings emerges from the communal grief cleansed. She feels that the grief has allowed her "to release all the accumulating weight of stolid living."(72) Yet her cleansing is a very distinctive cleansing: "she felt clean, strong enough to do anything, to carry any thing, any man who thought himself powerful enough to climb onto her." (72) Her mourning, her cleansing, has, in a sense, wiped away any internalized normative expectations concerning her gendered identity, that which might be expected of a woman by both the Tetsot'ine men and the English men, both Broadface and Back.

Broadface is beautiful to Greenstockings, but his face is still that of a man. While making love, Broadface hisses in Greenstockings' ear that he is looking for a son. She wants nothing to do with this, and throws him off. She says to him: "At least your words are big." (73) In rage he draws his knife, but she is too quick, already poised with a knife between his legs: "no man is quicker than a woman." (73) The hunter's knife is no match for the knife that skins, the knife that can easily castrate the man and reduce his power to simply words. Broadface continues with words, words which are designed to performatively bring about that which the norm of female subservience requires: "You're my woman.... You'll want me, you'll be moaning for me again." (73) Greenstockings responds with contempt: "Words.... Always your big words." (73) Men and big words.

Broadface and Back are alike as men. As Back stares at her, Greenstockings thinks of the time he tried to take her. Back, like all the other men, would like to take her. Back is brave, and he sits in his canoe "with his head so high." (74) Yet, Back's phallic power is like Broadface's words, powerless, helpless before the knife. Or so Greenstockings hopes.

Greenstockings hopes the English are dead before they kill everything here. Keskarrah responds: "You're just a woman," adding that "every woman knows what she knows." (75) He agrees with her in her assessment of the English, agrees with her knowledge: "I don't understand how we'll be able to live in our world with These English." (75) They bring along all this stuff, attached to their possessions which keep them from experiencing radical loss. And they are "always making marks, marks on paper that any drop of water can destroy." They are always depending on the word to still the restless forces that might bring about a plunge into the abyss. "They always have to hold something in their hands, something to make marks on, or to look at things or through knowable instruments." (75)

Keskarrah dreamed that Greenstockings would be a woman. She came from between her mother's legs: "And there you were, a small bloody body not wanting to come out between your mother's legs. Where I had already been quite often." (76) Keskarrah recognizes the knowledge of Greenstockings as a woman's knowledge that he too has accessed through dreaming. And that knowledge has its origins in the mother, so that if he has been able to partake in it through his dreaming, it is because he has been in the mother, in the same place that Greenstockings has been, and, as we shall see, wants to return.

Birdseye is not so sure of Keskarrah's participation. She says: "For men, women are *just* places to go, go in and go out." (76) Keskarrah does not believe that this is what he has done. He says that "women are the place of living and men want to be there too, then they are both truly alive." (77) However, Keskarrah believes that fathers have a privileged position over that of the daughter in relation to the mother: "Women just come out of there, but a father is always first inside a mother, children understand that." (77) According to Keskarrah, men want to go in and women want them to because that is the source of longing, of a desire which keeps things alive. Although the daughter's desire for the mother is analogous, Keskarrah believes that the male's desire is to be given priority in speaking of desire in general. In the last instance, desire is to be defined by the father's right to be first.

Keskarrah believes that the mutual desire between men and women in the Tetsot'ine world is different from the desire of the

English: "These English are human, but they are...different. As if they could travel all their lives without needing women to live." (77) Keskarrah considers himself as a Tetsot'ine male, as a Tetsot'ine father, to be different from the English.

Yet, Greenstockings objects to Keskarrah's comments, claiming that the English do not live without women. She says that "they just take women anywhere they travel." (77) To Greenstockings this is what is to be expected of all men, where women are just places to go in and out. So, whereas Keskarrah has tried to differentiate the Tetsot'ine male desire, and his own in particular, from the English male desire, Greenstockings and Birdseye see the two desires as the same.

Birdseye, with a woman's knowledge, sees what is happening with the English, especially with their instruments, their technology: "Maybe through those instruments the sun lets them see how the world is. For them always there, always the same." (78) Keskarrah is "dumbfounded." (78) He had never considered that the instruments were deceiving, and he did not in particular consider the way in which these instruments "might make [his] world more fixed than his own awareness could recognize." (78) If the sun lets the English see the world in its permanence, then the sun deceives, because the world that the Tetsot'ine live and thrive in is always changing, part of the longing, part of the mourning and then the longing. And the power of the sun that the English harness can deceive. In particular, the power of Richard Sun, the doctor, can deceive. Just as Keskarrah has been deceived by the power of the instruments, so now he is deceived by the power of English medicine.

This is what Greenstockings sees anyway: "if he [Keskarrah] does not believe in the power of These English, why does he go every day to Richard Sun for another portion." (79) The portion of salve that he hopes will cure the illness Birdseye has acquired, even though that very illness was brought by the English.

And as she applies the salve to her mother's face, Greenstockings realizes that her present relationship with her mother, where she applies English medicine to an English disease, is so different from a previous relationship with her mother. It is so different "from the memory of lying against Birdseye's back under the furs of the animals." (79) Back then, "when they were all the furry animals sleeping, dreaming together curled together skin to skin." (79) Back then, "she was a skin of happiness folded into exquisite awareness within sleep."

(79) These memories of her mother contrast with her later experiences with men, none of whom "has ever again helped her remember such anticipation." (79)

These feelings of maternal care are feelings Greenstockings felt "as an unthinking child." (79) She longs for that kind of thinking again where "she can think of...nothing." (79) Is this desire for the mother a regressive infantilization of Greenstockings as subject? Or, alternatively, is she returning to an imaginary point zero, where new possibilities for subjectivity can be conceived? More generally, does the return to the mother represent a foreclosing of access to the ground of desire in the non-object, closing down the route to new possibilities for desire, or is the return to the mother the very route by which the ground of desire in the non-object is accessed, thus allowing new possibilities for desire?

———•◦•———

Judith Butler can again help us, this time in making sense of the role of the imaginary. In her article "Arguing with the Real" (1993) Butler claims that the work of Žižek ends up "foregrounding the symbolic law and the real, and backgrounding the imaginary." (188) Before we pursue Butler's critique we should specify exactly what is meant by the concept of the real.

The concept of the real comes from Lacanian psychoanalysis (see Lacan 2002, Fink 1995, and Dean 2000). The real is that which is both prior to the expression of symbolic language and which emerges when symbolic language fails. In a sense, the development of the subject in symbolic language is made possible by an endless misrecognition of the real for what we more commonly call "reality." We are so reliant on our linguistic and social version of "reality" that the entry of the real into our lives is radically disruptive. All of our linguistic and social structures necessarily fail in relation to the real.

The real is so elusive to our understanding because it emerges in the experience of the subject only after his/her subjection to symbolic language. This experience of the real occurs through a break in symbolic language. It is when symbolic language breaks down for the subject that the subject experiences the real.

How then do we gain knowledge of the real as a critical force? The specific psychoanalytic answer coming from the Lacanian tradition is that we gain experience of the real through a special type of object: the *objet a*. *Objet* is French for "object" while *a* refers to the

French word "*autre*," meaning other. Therefore, with the *objet a* we have "the object of the other." The *objet a* is an object of desire which is radically other to our everyday reality and our everyday self. It is thus no ordinary object, but an object that is strange and unsettling to our usual sensibilities.

The value of the *objet a* is that it has no inherent relation to "reality" and, more specifically, reality as expressed in the present normative order. Desire for the *object a* in relation to the real is a desire that places us in contact with the **void** or **lack** that is the ground of Being. This means that we as subjects do not control the *objet a*; rather, the *objet a* is **always already lost** because as it expresses itself it immediately cuts away from the control of the subject who desires it. Due to its power of attraction the *objet a* elicits the desire of the subject but is immediately cut away from the subject into the real such that we could say that the subject does not really control the object but the object (in its relation to the real) controls the subject. A common response of our society to the experience subjects might have of objects being cut away into the real is to domesticate these strange objects by replacing them with normatively acceptable objects of desire. To counter this, psychoanalytic criticism seeks to highlight and emphasize the relationship of the subject to these strange objects that exceed the symbolic order.

To return to Butler's critique, the standard Lacanian presentation views the symbolic law as subversive of a fixation on image-constancy engendered by the imaginary. By subverting imaginary illusions, the symbolic law places us in contact with the real, that which is unsymbolizable, and because of this, the source for ever new productions of language and desire within the symbolic. It is not that the symbolic directly hits the real. Symbolic forms hit the real indirectly, through their subversion of the imaginary. And it is not that the real is the source of desire. Hitting the real, if only indirectly, opens the space for new forms of desire within the symbolic.

In contrast to this perspective, Butler wants to highlight the work of the imaginary in relation to the real and oppose what she sees as the Lacanian emphasis on the relation between the symbolic and the real.

Some Lacanians might claim that Butler misconstrues Lacan's notion of the imaginary. However, I think she does so for productive, and possibly, strategic reasons. In *The Psychic Life of Power* (1997), Butler refers to the imaginary "as the permanent possibility of misrecognition, that is, the incommensurability between symbolic demand ... and the instability and unpredictability of its appropriation." (96) Symbolic identity is "derailed in the imaginary" and thus "the imaginary signifies the impossibility of the discursive – that is, symbolic – constitution of identity." (96, 97) There is subsequently an equation made between the imaginary and the unconscious where the unconscious is understood as "that which thwarts any effort of the symbolic to constitute sexed identity coherently and fully, an unconscious indicated by the slips and gaps that characterize the workings of the imaginary in the unconscious." (97)

This seems to be a reversal of the standard presentation of the imaginary by many Lacanians, where the imaginary and the process of misrecognition are associated as stabilization of identity into a coherent whole that wards off awareness of the real. As I said, though, this reversal could be done for productive purposes. If Butler wants to shift the analysis away from the relationship between the symbolic and the real (with the imaginary ignored), and toward the relationship between the symbolic and the imaginary, things change quite a bit.

For Butler, the symbolic is a historically specific set of norms or laws that foreclose and abject certain possibilities for the subject. The imaginary represents the taking up of those possibilities denied by the symbolic within a specific political practice. Take homosexual love. If homosexual love is foreclosed and abjected by a reigning historical symbolic, then affirming homosexual love represents an imaginary turning to those lost potentialities of love denied by the oedipal dynamic of compulsive heterosexuality.

Instead of the lost possibility of homosexual love we might highlight here the lost possibility of the mother's love. It then becomes possible to view the plural forms of identification made possible by the bonds of attachment in the maternal, and the problems that ensue when those forms of identification are denied expression, as an imaginary base for later resistance to the symbolic norm. Although Butler herself does not highlight this connection of the imaginary and the maternal, the logic of her argument can certainly lead in that direction.

Here, we can in some way see a rehabilitation of the notion of the real, now no longer in alliance just with the symbolic, but with the imaginary as well. It also means that we rethink the bonds of attachment that are part of the maternal, not as leading to an imaginary misrecognition that thwarts a relationship with the openness of the real, but as an imaginary misrecognition that is directed to the constraints of a particular dominant symbolic, and one that thus allows for a productive relationship with the openness of the real.

These reflections of Butler seem to be at odds with the particular form of Lacanian thought endorsed by Žižek. Žižek, in *The Fragile Absolute* (2002), highlights a radical cut from a world of imaginary identifications, and seems to endorse a particular form of sacrifice that can only come through the symbolic. Imaginary forms of identification, like those that flow from the attachment bonds of the maternal, prevent an encounter with what Žižek calls the traumatic event of love. The issue of trauma is very important because Žižek believes that traumatic experiences herald a break in the symbolic chain which has the beneficial effect of providing us with an encounter of the real and the possibility then of subjectivizing the trauma without rendering us psychotic.

In a sense, Butler and Žižek agree that possibilities emerge through a break in the symbolic. However, for Žižek, the break with the symbolic has already been prepared for by a break with the imaginary. It is this double break in the form of trauma that allows the subjects in their destitution to experience in a radically contingent way the real. For Butler, the break in the symbolic is aided by an appeal to the imaginary where an encounter with the real occurs when the symbolic is derailed by the imaginary.

Thus, if we can say that Greenstockings experiences her relationship with (some) men as traumatic (her constantly being taken), then her attempt to turn to the memory of her mother would constitute, in Žižek's eyes, a misdirection, one that flees from an encounter with the traumatic real. However, if Greenstockings' return to the memory of her mother is a return to an imaginary image that allows her once again to retrieve lost possibilities of love, then the effect is not a misdirection, but in fact a movement toward the openness provided by an encounter with the real. This return to the lost possibilities of love in the maternal is important in understanding the unfolding relationship of love between Hood and Greenstockings. This raises the possibility of thinking of their love as a love that recaptures the lost possibilities of maternal love and by so doing places them in contact with the real as a source of freedom.

4 STRANGE GENDER

As I mentioned in the Introduction, the relationship between Robert Hood and Greenstockings takes peculiar routes, and one effect of these routes is the unfolding of unstable and precarious gender identities for each that rub against any normative understanding of masculine and feminine. This chapter will flesh out the implications of this emergence of a strange gender, by engaging with Judith Butler's explorations of gender in her work *Antigone's Claim* (200). The engagement with Butler will allow me to productively entertain alternative forms of gender construction that are able to consistently resist that which is normative, not only for the English and the Tetsot'ine at the time of the Franklin Expedition, but for Canadian culture today as well. In the context of the relationship of Hood and Greenstockings, I will propose the idea that northern love invites the possibility of a strange gender.

———✦———

Hood suddenly appears in the family lodge of Keskarrah while Greenstockings is webbing snowshoes. He says he wants to draw her while she works. Hood points at Greenstockings, and "gestures a fluid shape lightly in the air with his hand." (81) Despite the disdain for English instruments, and in particular English drawing, which attempts to create permanence out of change, to stem the flux, Greenstockings likes Hood's hand: "so long-boned and pale, so quick that the pencil it holds between two powerful fingertips sighs grey lines out of the bending paper." (81)

Hood's drawing, his production of the image, his gaze, is different from the rigid, fixing gaze of the English. As before, when he took Greenstockings' hand and drew his name in the shape of his head, Hood's hand moves from gesture to paper with an embodied sigh. Greenstockings, whose desire was closed to men, is now open to Hood: "A curve of her knee, her leg, appears." (81) He is so very unlike the men whom she does not desire: "he is so thin, so stretched and gaunt, so obviously helpless." (82) If all desire returns to the mother, a return that leaves us like children, helpless, then possibly Hood's unmanly helplessness makes him desirable, unlike the manly men who simply want to go in and out aggressively. In the face of such helplessness, Greenstockings wonders what would make Hood strong: "would good, rich food make him strong enough...to be interesting?" (82) Food prepared in the family lodge with the animal furs in a womb-like pot, a food from the mother, will make him strong, with a strength unlike that of the manly men.

Hood, of course, cannot communicate with Greenstockings by words, and he derives an intense pleasure from this: "it is enough for him that the meanings of their two incomprehensible languages pass each other unscathed in the close warmth of these hide walls." (83) Unscathed, because the meanings are not fixed and ordered but are contained by the maternal, the warmth of the lodge. This is so different from the words written in the "cold mud-smeared logs of the officer's quarters" (82) of the English, where Franklin and Richardson and Back "write down every English word they can think of." (82) Hood realizes that he has fallen into an unfathomable freedom.

Greenstockings' desire is excited, but she is, at the same time, troubled by that excitement. It seems that the desire she has unleashed is a necessarily troubled desire: "She cannot believe this thin, bony English can exist here: if she lets him love her, she will kill him." (84) Hood's love for Greenstockings will kill him, bring him death.

What kind of death? Birdseye still thinks Hood is Snow Man: "...Snow Man, Snow Man, white as snow man...why have you come?...what follows you...nothing but snow, nothing but woe man."

(84) Greenstockings' love is a love for Snow Man, a love for an unmanly man who brings on woe and is woe-man. Greenstockings says that if Birdseye insists on viewing him as snow, this makes it all the more important for her to love him, so that she can "hold him within herself" (84) even though he is already dead and gone. Yet, "he is certainly alive at this moment." (84) A moment where "she could thread him like this snowshoe." (84) Greenstockings' love is for an unmanly man who is both dead and alive at the same time. One who could become like the snowshoe.

Keskarrah agrees to Hood's sketch, and then he talks, telling a story which is an image of the land as an animal, a fish. Keskarrah talks "as if it were his voice that is drawing his outline from the white paper." (86) A voice can draw, a story creates an image. The word is an invitation for an image. He says: "the lake you named 'Winter' is really a fish with its head to the east and its tail whipping up the froth of rapids just below us, the place you've tried to draw so often already." (86) The fish is trying to swim away, to the east: "That's why the last trees here grow so large: that giant fish tries to swim east, but these giant trees hold it back, no matter how hard it swims, it can't move." (86–87)

Keskarrah then refers to the snowshoes Greenstockings is making. "they could carry you around [the lake]…Then you might be able to see." (87) If Hood, the Snow Man, becomes the snowshoe then he will be able to see correctly. And his seeing correctly would allow him to draw correctly: "If you drew the lake as it is you would have to see the fish, and you could name it correctly." (87) The implication is that the English naming, the English word, is not related to a correct seeing.

These reflections by Keskarrah on seeing and drawing relate directly to Hood's drawing of Greenstockings, who makes the snowshoes and who will make Hood the Snow Man into a snowshoe. Hood turns to Greenstockings and "is trying to find her shape before he attempts details." (87) He knows that "his fingers must imagine her shape since he cannot yet imagine physically uncovering her and actually seeing skin." (87) Then he says with words what he desires: "you are such a woman…." (87) And proceeds to draw those words of desire. He "draws this stunning woman's line from his fingertips over and over again; he can fondle her until he has found her body's exact turn, until he knows it so indelibly that when he slashes the snowshoe across her lap it seems he has hurled himself, dived across her lap stretched out and pointed, become the long fish-like shape he aches with her to be. Thrashing." (88) Gesturing, saying, drawing, and Hood becomes the fish that Keskarrah said he might be able to see. He has seen the fish, he has become the fish.

Given that Hood has learned to correctly draw, Greenstockings "believes [he] ... may be able to understand her fingers and her father." (88) He will be able to understand the story of the beginnings of the world, told by Keskarrah.

Sky and Earth came to lie together creating ground, which "is nothing more nor less than their happiness together." (89) Out of that happiness came moss and trees and fish and caribou, and then on the fourth day, man. The woman on four legs, the great bear, caught the man, but he escaped from her den to create the great river and the Everlasting Ice. Keskarrah says this is a story about "woman and man lying together...like bears." (89) Bears "will lick you tenderly because they want no more than what they already have." (89)

Then there is a shift in the storytelling, a turn to the fall from want to desire. Keskarrah says that "man does not have an endless bone like a bear ... something got mixed up for the man, somewhere, and he can't." (90) He can't stay inside the woman, the mother, and so he escapes. When he escaped from the great bear he was alone, alone with little to eat, hungry, feeling great absence and deprivation. And he sank always into the snow. Yet, he dreamt that he could run over the snow "as easily as the animals, as swiftly as wind smoothing it, whispering among birch." (90) So he turns to the birch trees and strips them into large hoops. But in the centre of the two strips was a hole, a huge absence. Every animal could easily run from him.

In his shelter, while he was gone hunting, a ptarmigan was busy working on the snowshoes, "their sad emptiness half woven over with babiche." (91) The ptarmigan would fly out the opening at the top of the shelter when he approached. To prevent her flying out again, before he left in the morning he sewed the opening closed. When he caught the ptarmigan "it turned into what he had often dreamed: someone like himself but o so different!" (91)

Then the two, the man and the woman, are able to return from absence into presence, the presence of the mother. They were "lying together hot as bears and children for ever." (91) For it was the woman who "alone could fill the frames he had dreamed and bent." This changed him, away from loneliness and absence; she provided for him "frame and woven center." (91)

This story represents an escape from the maternal only to return to the maternal. Keskarrah sings that "long ago, my mother told me this story of beginning ... O my mother, long ago my mother." (91) His mother told him about the escape from the den of the bears, but also from the original lying together of sky and earth, the sky in the earth forever, licking.

———◦•◦———

Perhaps the cutting of ties to the mother is also an escape of the word from the flesh. The subsequent loneliness and absence create a longing for return. The severing of word from flesh, word from image and thing, creates a desire for the word to be reunited with the flesh, the image and thing, for the word to be once again in communion with the thing. Hood appears as a Christ-like figure whose sojourn in this land is an allegory for the possible (re)uniting of word and flesh. Certainly, Greenstockings, in identifying with Hood's lack, seems to be identifying with him as a kind of suffering Christ.

David Savran, in *Taking It Like a Man* (1998), sees the identification with a Christ-like loss as a form of identification which is tied intimately with forms of masochism, both Christian and feminine. He sees these forms of masochism emerging strongly in various prominent countercultural movements in the U.S., from the Beats through to the Robert Bly–inspired men's movement. The identification with the suffering Christ allows for a divestiture of phallic values and an attempt to return to an open space of desire. However, Savran believes that, at least in the American experience anyway, this divestiture of an oedipal masculinity (represented by a controlling and over-bureaucratized father), leads to an attempt to return to a kind of frontier masculinity that is free to do as it pleases, especially to women, outside of any law-like structure that might constrain. According to Savran, what we then witness is the return of the phallus, an often aggressive masculinity that is now allowed to do violence without fear of penalty. And the hope is that this cleansed masculinity will be desired by all the women for its undomesticated virility.

Is that what is transpiring in Greenstockings' identification with Hood as a suffering Christ? Is Hood's unmanly suffering an attempt to shed the vestiges of the oedipalized world of the English society as reflected in the English masculinity of the Expedition? Is his encounter with lack and loss only a first move, after which is a movement into an aggressive and virile frontier masculinity?

I do not think so. Hood's encounter with loss is a quite different kind of loss than that outlined by Savran concerning the American experience, because it is bound up with a return to the mother. That is why ultimately Hood must be sacrificed, facing a Christ-like fate.

Kaja Silverman, in her essay "Masochism and Male Subjectivity" (1992), quotes approvingly from Deleuze's work on masochism, to suggest that the unravelling of male subjectivity and the movement into feminine masochism hinges on the return to the mother and an alliance between the son and the mother against the father. The father fails miserably to provide identification for the son and subsequently the son revels in an identification with the mother. In *World Spectators*, Silverman associates this paternal failure with a failure of the word in relation to the image. As the word-presentation fails in its attempt to control and conquer experience, the image or thing-presentation allows for an abundance of affective transfers.

Hood's Christ-like fate is one that witnesses the unravelling of the paternal English word and an encounter with the maternal Thing. How do we interpret the son's rebellion against the father and the subsequent pact with the mother against the father? And how should we interpret Greenstockings' rebellion against the father (Keskarrah) and against men (both English and Tetsot'ine) and her identification with the position of the son (Hood) as suffering Christ?

There is another question that arises from Keskarrah's story and its application to the love of Hood and Greenstockings. Could we not interpret the story's reference to the man's need for the woman as a conservative move, one that attempts to recoup the heterosexual norm in the face of the explosion of desire and difference? Yet, Hood is not a normative man and Greenstockings is not a normative woman. So, if this story has the possibility of a conservative recouping, in the context of the contact between Hood and Greenstockings, in the context of the contact between Christian sailor, whose identity as English masculine subject is troubled, and Tetsot'ine woman, whose identity as a native feminine subject is troubled, this particular recouping has other possibilities that are less normatively familiar.

Judith Butler addresses the question of non-normative gender recouping in *Antigone's Claim* (2000). We might say that the institution of the heterosexual norm whereby men and women meet to consolidate their desire through difference presents itself as a symbolic law that seeks to reproduce its effect from generation to generation. According to Butler, there are two accounts that legitimate this passage:

a conservative Hegelian account and a conservative Lacanian account, accounts that can quickly become unravelled.

First, the Hegelian account. Butler claims that Hegel's reading of Antigone renders Antigone's defiance against Creon as a defiance based in a wayward femininity that must be contained by the state. The power of Antigone's defiance is one that deforms the idealized kinship structure that the state assumes. According to Butler, Hegel, in *The Phenomenology*, universalizes a kinship structure that is socially contingent. (6)

Antigone presents a problem because she assumes a form of power which is denied to her in the normative kinship structure of the state. She becomes manly, adopting a form of masculine sovereignty. Her opposition to the rule of Creon must take on the normative power that she opposes. She must assume the voice of the law in opposing the law. She must appropriate the voice of the very one she is defying. (8–10)

Yet, Hegel claims that Antigone cannot claim the rights of citizenship, because her future place as mother in the family structure does not involve recognition, or even the desire for recognition, which is the basis of citizenship. Kinship relations, unlike state relations, do not involve the desire for recognition. Antigone's non-normative desire for her brother does not constitute a desire because, for Hegel, relations between brother and sister are not governed by desire. (13, 14)

In Butler's interpretation of Hegel, the state only gains its existence through interfering with the bonds of kinship, especially those that might go wayward. In particular, it is the duty of the state to oppose women, because women are by nature apolitical, and will turn to action that perverts the rightful activity of the state. To act in the state is to act universally. The problem with women, and especially mothers, is that they act particularly, for example, in a mother's love for the son. In order for the normative order of the state to be reproduced, the mother must sacrifice her son for the state. According to Butler, in *The Philosophy of Right,* Hegel maintains that the mother cannot be allowed to appeal to the ancient law of the gods, a law that comes before the codification of written language, a law that is enigmatic and incommunicable in the confines of the word. (31–39)

Greenstockings is like Antigone in assuming a manly posture that is non-normative for both the English and the Tetsot'ine. Her love for Hood is like the love of a sister for a brother and like the love of a mother for a son. And if desire collapses into identification (aren't the two to be normatively separate: we desire that which we do not identify with, and we identify with that which we do not desire?) then Greenstockings assumes the position of the brother and the son.

And Hood is attempting to forestall his complete sacrifice to the state as a normative masculine subject in the English navy. His desire for Greenstockings is a desire and identification with the position of sister and the position of mother and a defiance of the normative rule of the father who seeks his sacrifice.

What about the Lacanian account? Butler believes that conservative Lacanian theorists tend to insist on the separation of symbolic law and social norm. Social norms are alterable, but the symbolic law has a universality to it that defies alterability. This is particularly true in the realm of desire, for conservative Lacanians, according to Butler, maintain that the law of desire is regulated by the oedipal drama, and in particular, the law of the father, which operates there. There is an insistence here that the law of the father is not the same as the position of biological and socially specific fathers. Yet, the law must hold. (15–20)

For Butler, the distinction between symbolic position and social norm does not hold, because the symbolic position is only a social norm in a different mode of appearance. It is simply rendered ideal, and its very ideality comes from the fact that its contingency has been made necessary. When some Lacanians declare "It's the Law" this is for her a performative utterance, one that actively grants a force to a law that is believed to be universal and non-contingent. This performative action represents an allegiance to the law, a desire for the law. (21, 22)

In relation to Antigone's actions, Butler wants to know what will happen to the legacy of Oedipus when the rules that Oedipus defies no longer carry the power and stability attributed to them.

The problem with Antigone, according to Butler, is that she lies at the threshold of a symbolic order which is awarded universality. Although the symbolic order is external to the subject, there is, according to the conservative Lacanians, no impossibility of escaping it. It is universal and contingent at the same time. It demands to appear for the subject, but it has no ground outside of itself. This is especially true of the oedipal drama: it is both universal and contingent. The law of the father cannot be escaped, yet this law only appears through substitution by real fathers. What happens when real fathers fail, sometimes deliberately? This cannot affect the universality of the law, because the law is not dependent on its contingent substitutions. Butler claims that here contingency is stripped of its contingency, stripped of the possibility of establishing variable norms for the pursuit of desire. (40–45)

Butler sees Lacan's reading of *Antigone* in *Seminar VII* as pointing to an enigmatic appearance within desire that is not oriented toward the good, something that intervenes in the good to derail it from its path. In this sense, Antigone represents a desire for something on the far side of the symbolic, something before the codification of the law in the word. According to Butler, Lacan believes that it is possible for humans to cross this limit, but not in order to produce durable forms for the life of the state. The problem with Antigone is that she crosses over the limit permanently. The unwritten laws which Antigone claims are ones that do not correspond to the types of exchange that are part and parcel of the symbolic order. Antigone's love for her brother is not communicable with the symbolic exchange of signs. This brings her into death, but this death comes, according to Butler, only because she has defied the contingent structures that define intelligible and acceptable living. And if Antigone counters this symbolic, perhaps it is because she is challenging the acceptable terms of livability that the reigning symbolic order articulates. (46–55)

If Greenstockings is a manly woman who desires and identifies with Hood, who is an unmanly man, and they both, in their desire and identification, seek to return to the mother, are they then not slipping into an unlivable space that cannot endure, that can only be momentarily assumed to be abandoned to symbolic necessity? Yet, perhaps the unlivability of their space is one that can only be momentarily assumed because the symbolic rule of the father is a contingent assumption of power that remains normative, and not because of the universal insistence of the symbolic rule of the father. In this sense, its prevailing is due to its ability to beat back the challenges to the contingent norms it asserts, not because it is universal and necessary. The love of Greenstockings and Hood may have to be sacrificed, but this sacrifice is not a necessary sacrifice, but one contingently mandated by a ruling symbolic. At the same time, and precisely because of its contingency, the love of Greenstockings and Hood may live on as an enduring possibility and an enduring challenge.

5 LOVE AND TRAUMA

As we shall see, Robert Hood both experiences intense love as he lies in the Keskarrah family lodge and relives extreme trauma as he lies dying out on the barrens. This chapter will explore the relationship between love and trauma by tracing the experience of Hood and then theorizing that experience through debates in psychoanalysis. I will critique Žižek's Lacanian emphasis on the productive connection of trauma and love in the form of subjective destitution. I will turn to Kristeva's notion of the imaginary father to provide an alternative explanation of this relationship. Finally, I will argue that the impact of love on trauma comes principally through an ongoing relationship of the masculine subject with both the imaginary father and the oedipal father.

＊＊＊

Greenstockings "cooks her favourite meal for Hood." (157) They are inside the cocoon of the family lodge, lined with the hides of animals, protecting them, "this warm circular place she has always lived." (158) Greenstockings stretches the deer stomach that is hung over the fire and is cooking the meal. She talks of cooking equipment and laughs. Laughing occurs often inside Keskarrah's family lodge, inside the circular protective womb. But Greenstockings remembers that laughing had always been with the women, and now it is done with Hood. Greenstockings does not laugh with the men, but she can laugh with someone who is not a man, one who is not a normative Tetsot'ine or English man. Despite often being angry at men, Greenstockings is now easily laughing in the presence of a man, a man who is not quite a man.

Greenstockings speaks freely about cooking instruments, and although "not understanding a syllable of any word" she says, Hood is able to respond to her "singing voice." (157) Maybe he understands her voice precisely because he does not understand her words. Hood responds to the sounds she makes and not the words: "the sounds she makes skim fondly about in his ears, sing, as every concentrated minute he watches her mouth." (158) Hearing a fondly skimming sound corresponds with movements of her mouth. This watching, this seeing, is borne out in drawing: "he has been trying to draw her lips for two days." (158) In particular, he wants to "catch that bottom curve" of her lips, "the tilt of the corners where the sounds she makes seem to catch sometimes like a quick surprise." (158) The sounds emerge from a place marked fundamentally by surprise. Resisting the demand for comprehension and understanding (of syllables, grammar), Hood tells us that "he does not want to understand any word she ever speaks" He experiences "the freedom of watching, of listening with incomprehension." (158) Surprise, freedom, and incomprehension "fills him with staggering happiness." (158) In a "warm place with indescribable smells there is no listable fact, not a single word." (158) He is held within an "enveloping physical containment, all thought, all necessary decision, all duty gone." (158)

The place of "endless duty" is the officer's cabin, which is "unheatable." (158) Where he is surrounded by "frost white as leprosy." (159) This is a place where "blades of cold slice him long and thin to his very bones." (159)

The intense happiness and pleasure Hood experiences in the Keskarrah family lodge is similar to the happiness and pleasure that Greenstockings experienced with her mother in this same lodge. This intimation of the warmth and protection of the mother allows Hood to return to his own mother. He says, "I'm so warm here with you, it's almost like...like sitting beside the fireplace in the manse kitchen

in Bury" where "my mother knits in winter." (159) Hood is returned
to his boyhood home and the freedom and pleasure nurtured in the
bosom of the mother, a place where he has a special communication
with his mother. He whispers to Greenstockings: "Only my mother
... calls me 'Robin'. Only when we are alone." (160) Alone with
Greenstockings is like being alone with his mother. Desire for Hood
is a desire to return to the mother, the source of all warmth and
comfort. The desire to draw Greenstockings, to make an image of
her and not a word, is a desire to re-image-ine his mother, and re-
image-ine the love that comes only from the mother.

Greenstockings is moved by Hood's strange communication.
She has a thought which she has never had before about a man: "she
will tell him anything", especially that which is "unspeakable." (160)
This is a distinct form of telling, one not communicated with words.
And the freedom she feels in their communication comes from his
"incomprehension." (160)

Greenstockings finds Hood "stupid," but this is a stupidity that
is directly linked to her freedom. This is because "he asks nothing,
demands nothing, forces nothing to happen with his possible male
domineering." (161) To Greenstockings it is "as if he isn't even a
man, though he certainly is that, she has felt it." (161) He isn't a man
in one sense, the aggressive, take-the-woman sense, but he is in another
sense, one she has felt. This manhood is one that is predicated on a
"quiet and patience." (161) A quiet and patient manhood is like the
dream consciousness of a hunter. Not the usual English hunter, or
the hunters that the Tetsot'ine have started to become, with their loud
and impatient guns, but the "hunter dreaming animals to come when
they want to." (161)

Hood, as an unmanly man, is not like an English man or a
Tetsot'ine man, "a piece of something to be groped for inside his thick
head." (161) Greenstockings is convinced that Hood does not think
like that. She is convinced that his manly presence is one structured
around an "undemand," one very much like the undemand of the
mother, her unconditional love. Her mother left her with the memory
of pleasure to which all experiences with men have paled in comparison. But now Greenstockings feels the presence of a man who comes
close to her mother, who alone has been able to bring her pleasure:
"the memory of his gentle tenderness, the kind of undemand he offers
her humming a desire within her...strange...strange." Hood is a
strange man, a man like a mother. Greenstockings, who is a strange

woman, and Hood, who is a strange man, are both in their strangeness mothers, who communicate to each other by being mothers.

The communication of mothers is best seen in winter and in relation to the animals. In the maternal lodge, whose circular warmth and protection comes from the animals. With Greenstockings and Hood becoming mothers to each other, the animals are present as mothers in the food. Greenstockings says that we see the animals "most often in winter because it is then that their stomachs taste so sweet on earth, sweeter than mother's milk." (162) She tells how her mother sang when she nursed her. And this singing continued when the meat from the animal was prepared in the winter lodge. Keskarrah, the father, acting like a mother, a maternal father, "chewed the meat tender and wet for me." (162) If the animal meat, tender and wet, is like the mother's milk, then the animal and the father are both extensions of the mother, as the primary source of goodness.

As the father chewed the meat for Greenstockings, her mother sang to the animals: "Give me your stomach, Sweet animal ... milk of earth ... chew it, milk it into my mouth; Feed me." (162) The animal's meat, the father's chewing, and the mother's singing, are all supplements for the original nourishment. Greenstockings says to Hood that she will sing that song for him, and she will chew the meat for him and feed him, and she will offer him her breast: "For you, I took this stomach...until it was full, here it is, cooked and smoked too, full and wanting to be eaten, you can eat and I will eat with you, our fingers feeding each other.... I could feed you now, should I give you my breast, should I sing?" (162, 163)

Hood sings too. He sings "the acceptable melancholy of the English manse knit into each cell of his personal, endless longing." (163)

> Drink to me only with thine eyes,
> And I will pledge with mine;
> Or leave a kiss within the cup,
> And I'll not look for wine.
> The thirst that from the soul doth rise,
> Doth ask...a drink... (163)

Hood's longing is for the contact of eyes and mouth. He longs to look with the eyes and kiss and drink with the lips. This alone will satisfy his thirst. This is why he is so intent on being able to see properly. Will he be able to properly draw Greenstockings' lips? The image of her lips speaking is related to the kiss and the thirst, the kiss of the mother and the thirst for the mother. After the feast which nourishes, Greenstockings offers Hood her breast.

Hood attempts to feed Greenstockings "with the silver spoon he has carried inside his clothes from England." (168) He desires to be a mother for Greenstockings, teaching her how to eat from a spoon, as a mother to a child. They both become children for each other, enjoying "this game of eating, together, learning with simple silly laughter what they have both done since before consciousness." (168, 169) In teaching Greenstockings to eat from a spoon Hood gets her to purse her lips into an "oo" shape. Yet, "not comprehending what he is doing," (169) he is in a state of not knowing, not knowing that he is "shaping his name as round and long between her lips to meet his spoon." (169) Greenstockings' mouth "opens to accept it." (169) By forming his name "oo" with her lips to accept the spoon, she is accepting his name. Here, the name emerges from the context of eating like children, laughing like children, not knowing, not comprehending.

Hood is brought back to his mother, who sang, "Who fed Cock Robin?" (169) He sees himself and he eagerly replies, "I, said the Fish...." (170) Then he sees himself on the frigate when he first entered the navy, and he recalls being given the spoon by his godfather. This extends a tradition where godfathers give you a silver spoon when you begin your career. Hood points to St. Bartholomew's knife on the spoon – tradition says that the saint died by the knife. Knife and spoon. Death and life. The spoon that feeds and leads to the singing of "Who fed Cock Robin?" and the knife that kills and sings "Who killed Cock Robin?". His mother changed the rhyme – from the standard "killed" to "fed" – and proceeded to feed him. But the tradition of the father, the English father, employs the knife, or something worse.

Greenstockings tells Hood that he must eat now: That he will not die by the knife. She says: "My snow friend, no knife waits for you." (171) He must eat now and rest. She says to him that later he will "walk and walk over our land until hunger meets you, but now I feed you." (171) Greenstockings sees that later Hood will freeze: "certainly cold will clutch and devastate him before anything else." (171) This places more importance on his last (real) meal in the warmth of the maternal – "Who fed Cock Robin?" – before he encounters a death wrought with hunger and freezing, before he encounters all that is not maternal. Before he is abandoned by the maternal and sacrificed to the paternal legacy of the English word – "Who killed Cock Robin?"

Now, though, he can happily eat what Greenstockings feeds him, the fat of the meat she has "shredded and washed in her own sweet saliva." (171) as a mother to a child, allowing for an ecstatic experience: "he has never sensed such texture in his mouth." (171, 172) At least not since being a child with his mother. Hood experiences an oral pleasure that can easily become dangerous. The pleasure of the mouth in eating and naming can become the danger of hunger. Greenstockings says: "There is a place in my mouth that is dangerous." (172) It is dangerous due to a lack of nourishment by the mother. In that dangerous place, people get thin and think slowly, and can be reduced to eating those who have already died. Rather than eating from each other, they eat each other. This is not a solution, because it increases the hunger: "you just eat the hunger that has already eaten them." (172) To Greenstockings, hunger is terrible: "Hunger makes People crazy sometimes." (172) The battle to the death is a battle that arises from a lack of maternal nourishment.

Greenstockings tells Hood that in order to not go crazy you need to sing and to watch the ravens and the compassionate wolves. The wolves "taught us how to hunt these honey animals [the caribou] that feed us." (173) The wolves are our "brothers and sisters, we will never kill them." (173) Keskarrah has told her that if people are hungry they need to watch the ravens, who will lead the hunter to what the wolves in their kindness have left behind. For "we are all animals, we know our hunger, and when we have food we leave some for each other." (173)

Although not understanding the literal meaning of the words Greenstockings speaks, Hood understands at another level, the level of the dream. So he looks into Greenstockings' eyes and he can see the shape of the silver wolf he has already dreamed of earlier. Hood dreams that he is trying to draw the wolf. He is drawing in identification with the wolf, as he wants to draw Greenstockings, who now resembles the wolf. Yet, suddenly in his dream the quill is replaced by the gun and he shoots the wolf's jaw away. He is suddenly very sad – he does not understand how he could have shot the wolf. He has always refused the gun (except for that one time when he tried to duel with Back). He had, as an officer, been required to carry one, but he never loaded it, preferring the loaded quill. But now identification with the wolf, which sustains life, is replaced by gunning down the wolf, which destroys life. Even though he has not carried the gun himself, in the end, Hood is the one who carries the gun for the English, and is the one condemned for the destruction wrought by the gun.

With Hood lying in her lap, Greenstockings picks the lice from his hair, lice that are everywhere here. The English hate the lice. But Greenstockings patiently picks them one by one from his hair, opens her mouth, crushes them in her teeth, and then swallows them. Unlike the other English men who are revolted by the lice, and certainly would be revolted by someone eating them, Hood now finds that Greenstockings' work represents a "tender, intimate cleanliness." (175) His mother has claimed that this "is Next to Godliness." (175) Greenstockings explains that the lice live by drinking human blood. As she says this blood drips from her lip. As lice eat human blood, human blood is then eaten by humans as they eat the lice. This is an eating of the human that is nourishing, unlike the eating of humans racked by hunger. Which is more revolting? Hood understands: "We are all always bloody," he thinks. (175)

There are, then, quite different experiences of blood, two quite different ways in which blood can be shed. Hood is sent back in his imagination to the English ship where he has once again been forced to have his gun loaded against the sailor's mutiny. He is told he will have to execute them, shed their blood. And as he recalls this, he hears "the thin ascetic voice of his father, the Right Reverend Richard Hood," who speaks the lesson from St Paul in "his categorical, logical clarity of preposterous faith." (176) He recalls his father saying: "And all things are by the law purged with blood; and without the shedding of blood is no remission of sin." (176)

Yes, we are all blood and we all shed blood for each other, nourishing each other in turn. We are then bonded together in communion where the drinking of blood means a sustaining of life. But a sacrificing of ourselves through the maternal connection is different from another kind of sacrifice, a sacrifice of the scapegoat so that there will be a remission of sins, a distinctive form of paternally sanctioned sacrifice that is required by the words of his own father. This means that Hood will not only be sacrificed by the generalized English father, for the generalized English father's sins, but also, more specifically, by his own father, his own father's sins. It was his father who handed him over, at the age of fourteen, to Franklin's command.

Hood, realizing all of this, is in despair at the way in which his paternal heritage has shaped the blood-connection. He desperately seeks a return to the mother. He clutches Greenstockings and then "her folded legs loosen about his face." (176) And as he, for the moment, experiences the comforting return to the mother, Hood is overwhelmed with a feeling of mutuality, and communion with Greenstockings. He removes the boots which Greenstockings herself had sewn for him, boots that had made him feel powerful, just like the snowshoes. Then he pulls his stockings down and offers them to her. Greenstockings removes her moccasins and "he watches her leg, her skin, slip down and fill the space only he has shaped." (177) She stands up in his green stockings and he feels toes "spreading like fingers into the gentleness of wool." (177) Her feet were "sheltered and safe within the interwoven circles knit so lovingly by steel in the hands of his loving mother." (177) In the safe and secure family lodge, protected by the hides of animals, Greenstockings and Hood feed each other food from the animals. Hood has been sheltered and protected by the stockings sewn by his mother, and the boots sewn by Greenstockings. After shuddering at the paternal heritage that performs a distinctive sacrifice of life and a distinctive shedding of blood, he now experiences a quite different sacrifice and a quite different taking of blood, one that provides for a communion. He responds by giving the gift of warmth and protection provided by the mother.

And then Birdseye murmurs in dream-consciousness the fate of Hood as Snow Man. She begins to spastically sing English words from the rhyme "Who killed Cock Robin?": "Cock...robin...rock... robin...who...saw...him...I...said...the fly..." (178) She goes on, "With...my...little...eye..." (179) Whereas Hood had earlier dreamt of his own mother's "Who fed Cock Robin?" now he hears Birdseye dream of his other fate: "Who killed Cock Robin?"

Later, destitute out on the barrens, Hood prays, "what may befall me this day O God I know not but I know that nothing can...." (220) The prayer ends there and does not move on to "separate me from your love." Hood has been separated from the love of the father, and he doesn't know what will happen to him while being separated from this love. He has experienced the love that can only come from the mother, but has never experienced that maternal love from the father. Hood is physically exhausted now, but this is combined with a psychic exhaustion, an exhaustion both initiated and prepared for by the absence of love.

The Expedition is returning from the Polar Sea, trying to return to Fort Enterprise over the barren lands and not by river. Franklin and Back and others have gone ahead and have promised to return with food to the three Englishmen remaining on the barrens – Richardson, Hepburn, and Hood. They are joined suddenly by a fourth man, the Mohawk, Michel. Michel, along with Belanger, is sent back to Richardson's group to help. Yet, Belanger is not with Michel. Michel claims that Belanger did not follow him. To the three English men, Michel "seems suddenly very powerful:so deliberately intense and muscled." (222) And he is carrying "a long rifle with powder and shot." (222)

They are also astounded that Michel has brought meat. The three English men have dreamed of food. They dream of seeing a Raven who will lead them to food. They say, though, that they would give up four roasted pigs for a "great hot fire." (224) Hood recalls a biblical scene: "Three men bound in the midst of the burning fiery furnace." (224) He says that they could be like the three men who "could walk loose in the midst of it" without "a hair of our head singed." (224) Richardson adds that "there were four men in the fiery furnace." (224) Hood replies that yes, "also an angel, I pray, sweet angel, come! Carry us into the great, fiery furnace, the Yellowknives call it 'Like a Woman's Breasts', o soft breasts, blessed be God." (224) Hood, in the midst of bitter cold, longs for the presence of the angel in the fire who will offer him her soft breasts to soothe his pain. This is a return to the warmth of infancy and the soothing contentment at the mother's breast.

This fourth in the dream, the maternal angel, is very different from the fourth present now, the Mohawk Michel, who in his "miserable drudgery" displays "hatred on his full and twisted lips." (224, 225) Hood, starving and cold on the barrens, has sunk into a pleasurable dream space where the protection and care of infancy are present. Michel destroys this by offering him "small meat, scrawny juices" which "ruin once again Hood's accepted somnolence of starvation." (225) Michel has destroyed his fast and, in turn, destroyed the peace he has achieved.

For Hood, the presence of Michel is different than the presence of the angel. Hatred is different from love. And masculine anger in particular is different from what Hood knows to be maternal love. For Hood, the angel is clearly associated with Greenstockings. Hood dreams of Greenstockings at Fort Enterprise. She will be there, "fire

burning in that endlessly warm round lodge." (227) Hood prays,
"dear God my god ... bless her bless her that woman more gentle
and tender...." (227) The angel sent by God who provides gentleness
and tenderness is contrasted with Michel who seems so powerful.
Hood asks why Michel has come to him rather than the angel. Michel
does not know how to find Fort Enterprise. He is "lost crossing tire-
less rivers – sea coasts and rivers without trees." (228) Michel is lost
here as well, cast adrift from his secure moorings, and he is both
lost and angry.

Hood then thinks of trees and the appeal of trees. In contrast
to Michel, "the wrong kind of Indian" for this place, he thinks of
Keskarrah and the esker that shelters Keskarrah's family lodge. He
is associated with the trees, for it was Keskarrah who drew them to
the esker that would shelter the fort. Hood dreams of "branches piled
in warm green bedding over his lodge." Creating the secure womb
in which "arms fold him into warmth of breasts the apple taste of
her nipples, o sweetest sweetest." (229) Then Hood turns in his
dream-consciousness to the name of Jesus: "How sweet the name
of Jesus feels." (229) The comfort Hood has experienced from
Greenstockings in her family lodge forms the name of Jesus for him.
Belief in the name of Jesus is, at this point, inseparable from the
maternal experience. He refers to the arms of Greenstockings that
hold him as "her everlasting arms." (230)

Hood touches himself and "he feels bone." "Is there skin?"
he asks. (230) He thinks of his feet and the green stockings his
mother had made for him and he gave to Greenstockings. He says
that "his long green woolly feet ... they have gone." (231) There
are two kinds of green present here, one, the green stockings, in
reference to the mother, and two, the green of gangrene, in reference
to the cold and the snow. Both are present here, ambivalence in the
experience of green.

The green of gangrene has made his feet useless, and Hood
associates this with all those other things which are useless here on
the barrens: "they are useless anyway, all useless: books, instruments,
smashed canoes, feet, whole bodies ... sprawled over tundra, too bony
to eat." (231) This uselessness of his green feet is contrasted to the
green of Greenstockings who, in his dream-recollection, takes his feet
and "kneads them supple as the caribou leather covering her breast and
tongues them, each toe warm as milk, into the haven of her nest

and body." (231) The feet are useless with all those instruments, yet they become something else when embedded in the maternal nest.

Hood wonders now whether "they had clawed thousands of miles of sea and land and sea and back over the land again, to discover no more than each other's walking skeletons." (232) If the logic of the death drive holds sway here, are they not discovering spirit reduced to a bone? If we are to believe Žižek, and his interpretation of Hegel in *The Sublime Object of Ideology* (1989), life pared to the bone is the ultimate expression of spirit, the supreme encounter with spirit as the void, the nothingness that grounds all expressions of something. However, this idea of emptying the self to discover the self is not the end of the story for Hood, because he dreams of a return to the mother, to Greenstockings and the maternal lodge, a return that Žižek and other Lacanians of like mind would never dream of.

In fact, Hood realizes that the destitution of cold and hunger that has reduced his spirit to a skeleton was avoidable if the Expedition had recognized the image that Keskarrah "drew on the ground when they first arrived on the shore of the great crashing lake." (233) Keskarrah called this river the Ana-tessy and had indicated that it was "the closest and easiest river for their return if they must return from the east." (233) The trip back from the Polar Sea would have been made much easier, and they would have been able to avoid the destitution they suffered, if they had given credence to the image that Keskarrah had drawn. Instead, they attempted to travel over land using their instruments of navigation, ending up with "the confusion of after-the-fact numbers that foretold nothing ... all of Lieutenant Franklin's instruments and notebooks vanished in glaze." (233) These instruments and the calculations made from them were truly useless compared to the strength of Keskarrah's image.

Hood also realizes that this trek across the barrens, using instruments and numbers instead of the image, is represented by "his father's name. Drawn long across this land." (233) It is his father's name which has brought him to this point of destitution. Hood is not referring here to a universal destitution, reflective of the ultimate destiny of spirit, as Žižek and other Lacanians would have it, but a contingent destitution, an alterable starvation of spirit, which is the distinct legacy of the father's name. Not then the universalizing father's name, which is understood to be unavoidable and constitutive of all subjectivity, but a very particular father's name, his father's name, whose work was avoidable. It is a historically specific father's name: an English father, an English father's words, lacking the maternal connection. This is why Hood dreams of the mother, in horror at the father, his father, his English father.

Then Richardson begins to read from Leviticus the passages of the burnt offering which was condemned by God. One passage says that they "offered strange fire before the Lord." (234) And in response to this strange offering "there went out fire from the Lord, and devoured them." (234) The people are devoured because they cooked over the fire an offering which was false. What is the nature of this false offering?

Michel is cooking over the fire red meat and they eat "stringy meat from shreds of bone." (235) Although he claims that this is the remains of a wolf, Richardson is skeptical. Richardson is skeptical because he has an intimation that the meat they are eating is not a wolf's but that of Belanger, the voyageur who was to accompany Michel to them. He suspects that Michel has killed Belanger, carried his body to this place and stashed it, going out to the stash and returning with meat.

The experience of death by members of the Expedition comes through the death and sacrifice of the other. This is a death that is distinctly different from the death that comes when the animal gives itself up through dream, or when the wolf and the raven lead the human to food. It is a death that comes from the gun, that instrument Keskarrah and Greenstockings and Hood hate so much. Instead of eating meat that is properly sacrificed, we have here a false sacrifice, one that comes through murder by the gun.

The name of the English father which has led them here, a name emblematic of a culture of the word and the gun, has produced a sacrificial logic, not a universalized sacrificial logic where destitution allows for the openness of desire, but a particular, specific, individualized, sacrificial logic. There is, though, another form of sacrifice available, one that eats the meat provided willingly by the animals through the dream connection. This is a sacrificial logic where the subject becomes destitute in a return to origins, a return not to the gaping abyss, but to the embrace of the mother. One where the subject experiences the embrace of the father, not as name of the father, but as father-mother, the nurturing father, the father who has himself embraced the maternal connection.

If two forms of sacrifice can be distinguished here, how do we make sense of Michel's involvement? When Michel is informed by Richardson that Franklin's party probably has not arrived yet at Fort Enterprise, he becomes enraged. He says he will leave the three English here, that he should have never come back to help them. He is afraid he will die here with them, and that they will eat him. He says that when he is dead "he knows what they will do. They will eat him, the way they ate his brother on the Ottawa River, that is what Whites do to Mohawks, if you can't help them they just tear you apart and eat you – bones and all!" (239)

The murder of white Belanger and the eating of him come in the wake of an earlier trauma where the Mohawks have been eaten by the Whites. The destitution wrought here is continuous: eat the other or be eaten by the other. Not a mutual giving but a traumatically induced and murderous eating, born in the pain induced by a lack of love and continuing on in that vein.

Richardson, Hepburn and Hood are stunned by Michel's "unthinkable words." (239) They propose that Hepburn go with Michel to reach Fort Enterprise. Hood says that "we must not, sacrifice, him too." (239) The unthinkable words that Michel has uttered have allowed Hood "to utter at last the impossible word: *sacrifice*." (239)

The distinctive sacrificial logic of the English masculine subject is working its way through here. This is a logic that demands that sacrifice be tied to your duty as an English sailor. A duty that has sent them on the Expedition to chart the "numberless rivers and rocks and shorelines and lakes," but yet that duty has "helped them discover very little English vocabulary." (240) English words are helpless, destitute in this land, and the English are left with the impossible word: sacrifice. The English male subject, the English sailor in his duty, is reduced to nothing, "encircled by undifferentiated namelessness." (240) And all that is left to utter is the word 'sacrifice.'

How is this sacrificial destitution in which one is reduced to the void of namelessness different from the sacrificial logic operative in Keskarrah's lodge? In the lodge, Hood is returned to origins that are not a primordial lack of nameless nothingness, but a love and embrace of the maternal presence. In the face of the failure of the father's name, Hood is left destitute. But in his destitution on the barrens, where murder and eating the other are the response to trauma, he dreams himself back to Greenstockings' lodge, and to his mother's nursery rhymes. In response to the specific trauma of an unloving father, Hood experiences both kinds of sacrifice: both the sacrifice of the male subject to the void, a nameless nothingness experienced out on the barrens, and a sacrifice of the male subject to the maternal presence in Greenstockings' lodge.

These reflections may help us understand Michel's trauma and anger. Richardson and Hepburn have grown increasingly afraid of Michel's anger. Hepburn says that "strongest is the worst ... they can...kill you first ... when you're too weak...to protect yourself." (241) Hepburn knows that the strongest are the slaves, the paddle-slaves, who slave away for the master English. In Michel's case, we have a slave who is seething with anger over the murder of his brother by the Whites, who is traumatized by the cannibalistic annihilation of his brother.

Recognizing the superior strength of the slave, yet misrecognizing the anger as uncivilized nature, the English believe that only a strong hand can do. Richardson says that "Franklin was wise ... to send the strongest voyageurs ahead with Mr. Back." (241) Why? Because Back can control: "A leader must always...control...men, before they are uncontrollable." (241) The contrast between Back and Hood is again relevant. In these matters, Hood's unmanly traits are useless. Back is a manly man, "the smallest but strongest officer ... and certainly the quickest gun. And ruthless." (242)

The Franklin Expedition is, in a sense, on a mission of sacrifice, a death-wish, ordered by a historically specific death-drive. In their trek through the North, these strangers are looking for the non-object of desire which is the source of all desire. Yet, they can reach this source only through complete destitution. Is it only when one is com- pletely emptied that the non-object is discovered, where emptiness comes from a very material process of emptying (eating) each other? Certainly, Hood's plight seems to, at one level, reflect this pursuit. Yet, on another level, his plight points to a different search, for a different source, called love.

Žižek, in *The Fragile Absolute* (2002), speaks of a distinctive form of Christian love. This is a love that paradoxically comes through hate, hating your neighbour, specifically, hating his ego so that the death of the ego will save him. The love that Hood experiences is different from this. It is a love grounded in the maternal presence, one that moves not into namelessness but into childlike security. Is this dream of Hood's for childlike love an escape from the more real pursuit (in Lacanian terms, the pursuit of the real) that marks the true logic of sacrificial destitution? One where you face the trauma of the real head-on, without the sweet smell of maternal retreat?

As the particular sacrificial logic of destitution that the English Expedition embraces plays itself out on the barrens, Richardson reads Biblical passages. He reads passages of prohibition against uncovering the nakedness of the father, the mother, the sister, and the son's daughter. Hood suddenly laughs, much to the amazement of the others. He says, "My f-f-father ... never read...that...vespers!" (243)

Why would his father not read this passage? What form of foreclosure lies here? It seems that the father violated some norm of nakedness such that his reading of this passage constitutes an acknowledgement that the norm had been violated. Hood asks Richardson: "Is there anything, about a daughter's...nakedness, or a son's?" Richardson thinks: "what childhood abomination has Leviticus led this poor boy's dying memory back into?"

Hood's search has finally led him to this. Not to the traumatic real, the source of all desire, but to the reliving of a specific trauma about a father who is remembered as abusive. As he lies on the barrens, in a destitute skeletal nakedness, the floodgates open and he is pulled back to another time of nakedness, the nakedness of the son in the presence of the father. He remembers longing for the love of the father and feels strongly he was denied it.

This is the playing out of the English sacrificial logic of destitution for which Hood is the victim, the scapegoat for the father. And Hood is a victim and a scapegoat not only for his own father but for the English Expedition as a whole. Taking our cue from René Girard in *Violence and the Sacred* (1985), we can speculate that Hood might just be that one person who comes to bear all the sins of the Expedition, the sins of the English in the North.

Memories of his father bring Hood back to the familial scene on Sunday. The laughter he experienced when Richardson read the prohibitions against nakedness (which his father did not read) again grips him. He sees "his father reading that ponderous text so long after Trinity." (244) In a hallucinatory state he recalls fragmentary passages his father read from the book of Job, chapters 28 and 38 on the twentieth Sunday after Trinity. Why would his father, a priest in the Anglican Church, read the book of Job so long after Trinity? What his father read from the Scriptures would have been governed

by the Table of "Lessons Proper for Sundays" in the Book of Common
Prayer. On Trinity xx, this Table appoints chapter 2 of the book of
the Prophet Joel to be read at Morning Prayer, and chapter 6 of the
book of the Prophet Micah at Evening Prayer. Trinity xx falls in
October, while Job is read at daily Morning Prayer in June.

Hood's distress – his suffering, his fear, his pain – is leading
him to hallucinate the fragmentary passages from Job at the same
time as remembering a Trinity xx of his childhood. He hears his
father reading Job because these passages feel, to Hood, like the true
words of his father, the words of a father who has sacrificed his son.
Later, Hood searches for "the exact words and every detail of punc-
tuation … every iota frozen aloud into him that he is now condemned
to recall here in this mocking inescapable land, they burst blazing
as ice inside his head." (248) Some of the words are from Jonah,
chapter 4, but also from the rhyme "Who killed Cock Robin?" God
the father sends a worm to destroy the little shade Jonah has from
the sun. This is true for Hood in reverse: Hood is deprived of any
comfort from the cold. And again Hood sees "the thick words" of
Scriptures and remembers words from Luke 12, except that the passages are interspersed with the word "kill," which is not in the text.
The words of Luke 12 admonish men to empty themselves. In relation
to memories of his father, Hood experiences not a comfort following
emptiness but a killing of the spirit.

And at the same time, Hood recalls the nursery rhyme Robbin-
a-Bobbin. (250) He also recalls the reframe from "Who killed Cock
Robin?" (251) Nursery rhymes were rhymes of comfort when
remembering his mother, but with memories of his father they feel
like rhymes of killing – kill (Robbin-a-Bobbin) or be killed (Who
Killed Cock Robin?) This is the logic that now surrounds Hood out
on the barrens.

Hood tells Michel that he will not show him how to use the
compass. Michel leans close to him and hisses in his face: "I tell you.
I kill you, all the time, I tell you, before you die, I tell you I kill, you."
(251) Hood now knows that these are "words that have whispered
themselves into this landscape week after week through winter and
spring and the exhaustion of summer, until he recognizes them like
starvation." (251) The words "before you die" have eaten away at
him for nine months, ever since the time in Greenstockings' lodge
when Birdseye spoke those broken words of English, referring directly

to the Cock Robin rhyme. The despair he experiences now is centred on now knowing, in a state where "you have exhausted the last jot and tittle of suffering" (252), that you will be killed, even though this has been foretold long ago.

Hood is recognizing what was fatefully true all along, ever since those first traumatic encounters with his father. Hood feels like he was killed by the father then, but only knows it now at the level of self-consciousness. He has, in a sense, subjectivized the trauma, leading not to anything like curative enlightenment, but to pain and suffering because of the betrayal of love.

Yet, we certainly cannot leave things at that. For what we have articulated so far is the particular subjective state of Hood as depicted by Wiebe. It is a narrative of the son's complaint against the father and the alliance between the son and the mother against the father.

Perhaps, though, Hood's father has his own complaint in this story, a complaint that his son refused the hand of the father, preferring instead to cling to the mother and her love. This is then the other side of the register, one conspicuous by its absence in Wiebe's narrative, namely that the son, consumed with the maternal connection, refuses the paternal function, and in so doing continually refigures the father as a haunting presence, a monstrous figure from the real. Perhaps the son's continual return to the mother's love is a sign that announces his refusal to mourn the loss of an impossible father, and to reconcile himself with the everyday tragedy of the human father.

The conflict over Job is thus symptomatic of the feeling of a father spurned by his son and a son spurned by his father. And doesn't the father have a case here? Hasn't the son placed the father in the real as an impossible object? The father is expected to be just like the mother, only completely different. He is bound to fail on both counts: if he tries to provide maternal love, he pales in comparison to the mother, and if he tries to provide paternal distance, he suffers the complaint of abandonment. Thus in this scenario, it is all too easy for the impossible father in the real to turn into a monstrous figure from the real, haunting the son continuously. Is this what is going on in Hood's relationship with his father?

It is the issue of paternal distance turning into the complaint of abandonment that is important here. In essence, Hood turns paternal distance into paternal abandonment. The question is: was this necessary? My answer is yes, but my yes answer is a complicated one and in order to understand why we need to turn to the work of Julia Kristeva.

———•—•———

Kristeva has argued strongly for the importance of the imaginary father as a figure of identification for the child that is separate from the figure of the mother. (1987). What is not as strongly emphasized in the interpretation of Kristeva's work is her equal insistence on the presence of the oedipal father. This emphasis emerges more clearly in her recent two works on revolt. (2000, 2002)

Let's begin with the imaginary father. Kristeva (1987) wants to explore the relationship between love and narcissism, and to rescue the concept of narcissism from the negative position it holds in Lacanian thinking, where narcissism is a state to be overcome through the oedipal process. For Lacan, narcissism, as a form of self-love, is tied to the stable image established through mirroring, which allows the individual to misrecognize himself as a unity, a coherent self. And because mirroring is established exclusively through the mother-child dyad, the pre-oedipal relationship between mother and child, and the merging that is presumed to take place there, has often been referred to in the Lacanian tradition as the source for narcissism and the imaginary ego.

For Kristeva, narcissism needs to be distinguished from auto-eroticism. Narcissism is already a new action that supplements the autoeroticism of the mother-child dyad. In contrast to the Lacanian image of merging, narcissism represents an early presence of a third that comes in between the dyad. At the same time, though, it is a structure that precedes the oedipal ego, and even the mirror stage. (21, 22)

Narcissism appears as the first attempt to deal with the empti-ness brought about by the early experience of lack and absence. It is the first attempt to deal with emptiness through language, through the symbolic function, meaning that narcissism does not represent an absence of the symbolic, but rather its early presence. In this way, it represents the first separation between what is not yet a subject and what is not yet an object, meaning that subject and object are sepa-rated, but never clearly separated. (23, 24)

The structure of narcissism develops into an "amatory identi-fication" which rests on the assimilation of another person's feelings. The object the child identifies with is a strange object, one that is separate from him but incorporates elements of the oral phase where what he incorporates he becomes. It is not really a separate object he identifies with, but a model or a pattern to be imitated, where identification is not so much having, but being-like. Yet, rather than identification being opposed to the establishment of the symbolic, Kristeva claims that in identification the connection to language is important, because the binding to the other that occurs through identification is to the speech of the other, a speech which establishes a pattern to be imitated. Certainly, there is a kind of fusion here, but it is a fusion wherein the child is transferred to a new psychic space, a third realm, one that is still quite primal, one where he is able to chew, swallow, and nourish himself with words. (24–26)

Kristeva calls this emerging structure of narcissism the "imaginary father" in order to point to a third realm that is beyond the fusion of the dyad. This is, however, a strange father, one very different from the oedipal father. Kristeva maintains that when narcissism predominates, there is no awareness of sexual difference. Thus, the term "father" refers to both parents as embodiments of the ideals of fusion and separation. For there is neither mother nor father as logically separate objects, but an immediate, direct identification with a figure who nurtures both connection and separation. The connection is here to what Kristeva calls a "mother-father conglomerate," a relation to the mother and her desire for the other, for the outside world of language and difference. (26)

The imaginary father is the one who, through identification, returns an ideal image to the child, and therefore embodies what Freud has referred to as the ego-ideal. Although strongly tied to the child through identification, the imaginary father is still nevertheless an other not fused with the child. He nurtures the desires of the subject (rather than what Lacan describes as the ego) because they are not immediate requests or demands. (32, 33)

For Kristeva, the idealization of the other in love, the idealization of the imaginary father, gives rise to transference of the primal body to the position of narcissism. The idealized other is be distinguished from the autoerotic exchange between mother and child. A third party is introduced which becomes the condition for the life of the subject, for a loving life, one that is not built on fusion. In this connection, Kristeva distinguishes between two kinds of mothers, a clinging mother and a loving mother. The loving mother (not necessarily a biological female) is someone who has an object of desire outside of the child, a third who directs the desire of both the mother and the child to the outside. Without the relation to the third, the child will either hate the mother or cling to the mother. Clinging to the mother results in an inability to love that is tied to autoeroticism. The auto-erotic cannot allow himself to be loved except by a maternal substitute who clings to him, who is undifferentiated from him. (34)

It is through identification with an ego-ideal, rather than the super-ego celebrated by Lacan, which, for Kristeva, turns the ego into a subject. The ego becomes an erotic body that is transferred from fusion to the love of the other. And again, contrary to the Lacanian prejudice against identification and the ego-ideal, symbolic language is active here, because identification causes the subject to exist within the signifier of the other. There is a transference to the place of the other, what Kristeva calls a "metaphorical relation of love." (30) Metaphor implies a relation of substitution, where the fusion with the m/other is substituted with an ideal image or signifier established by language. This emphasis on metaphors of love contrasts with the importance Kristeva sees Lacan placing on the metonymy of desire. Metonymy implies a relation of displacement where our movement away from fusion with the m/other and into symbolic language means that we will be constantly displaced from one image or signifier to another image or signifier. According to Kristeva, it is the oedipal name of the father that, for Lacan, transfers us to such a symbolic process, a process which represents a clear break with imaginary fusion. Here, metonymy is understood to be more fluid and less fixed than metaphor, which still is stamped with narcissism and the imaginary. (29–31)

Kristeva wishes to rehabilitate the work of metaphor from the grips of Lacanian criticism. For her, the object of identification is a metaphorical object, a substitution for the maternal within language. This means that the idealized object is both distanced from the maternal, and yet still close to the maternal and the bonds of connection embodied there.

Yet, the emphasis on the imaginary father does not mean that the oedipal father is put aside. For Kristeva, the oedipal father is essential, especially in relation to the subject's separation from the archaic mother. We see this emphasis in her recent work on revolt.

Kristeva views revolt as tied to an overcoming of the archaic, in particular the archaic mother. Indeed, as her arguments develop in these works, it becomes clear that she understands revolt in decidedly paternal terms. Kristeva tells us that in order for revolt to be effective in securing freedom, there must be a confrontation with an obstacle, a prohibition, a struggle with authority and the law. (2000: 7) Referencing Freud in *Totem and Taboo*, Kristeva says that revolt's success comes through a displacement of the father's authority on to the sons, and the formation of a symbolic pact which protects the sons from the impurity of the maternal space. (21–24)

There are, however, two fathers for Kristeva, one imaginary and the other oedipal, and both are necessary for revolt, both necessary in securing a space of separation from the mother. The imaginary father is the father of identification and idealization, one who, through the effect of the mirror, presents the subject with an image of the ego that allows a space from the maternal container. Kristeva is at pains to emphasize the importance of this formation of the narcissistic ego for aesthetic representation, and surprisingly, for the emergence of the death drive. By loving itself, an image of itself, the subject engages in a kind of de-eroticization, a disengagement from the drive of Eros, thus exposing itself to the death drive. Kristeva comments that when "we invest not in an erotic object (a partner) but a pseudo-object, a production of the ego itself, that is quite simply its own aptitude to imagine, to signify, to speak, to think." (2000: 55) In its narcissistic withdrawal, the ego makes use of the negative, assumes the risk of the death drive, and forms a new object, which is not mommy or daddy, not an external object, but an internal object that is then capable of producing speech.

Yet, despite the importance of the imaginary father as a paternal structure, Kristeva insists that the paternal must be transformed through the figure of the oedipal father. Rather than separation through love, we now have separation in relation to the agency of the law: "I must identify in relation to the law at the same time as I separate myself from it in order to create my own place." (2000: 84) The figure of the oedipal father does not support me but threatens me with sanctions, puts in front of me his authority, as a block to my path. This authority is unique, however, because it is grounded in negativity: the oedipal father exercises his authority in the belief that he can lose it. He is both presence and death. He presents me with his authority but he also lets me know that I can displace him, put his authority to death.

This oedipal movement brings with it a form of freedom, one more radical than that associated with transference and the imaginary father. Yet there is a commandment associated with the law, in that once we subject ourselves to the prohibition, freedom can only come through its violation. Kristeva argues, citing Lacan, that separation brings about a freedom that is grounded in an ethics beyond the commandment. The subject with such an ethics is one whose "desire is not subject to a commandment outside itself." (2002: 227) The subject's commandment is one that raises the drive to a higher level, to the level of the death drive, a level beyond the constraints of the ego, and one that is bound to a subjective interiority that is radicalized.

On the basis of these considerations of Kristeva we could interpret Hood's flight back to the mother as one that is done in the context of his longing for the love of the father. Hood's father abandons him at the age of fourteen to the navy, and this is a double abandonment. It is an abandonment that denies him the love of the imaginary father and it is an abandonment that denies him the love of the oedipal father. In this sense, Hood is denied both the love provided by ideal identification and the love provided through actively struggling with prohibition and the law. His separation from the maternal presence is not aided by a father who is like the mother and is not aided by a father who is not like the mother. In the absence of these two aspects of paternal love, Hood's only outlet for love is a return to the archaic mother of his early childhood, the mother of warmth, coddling, and nursery rhymes. Yet, I think it is clear that, as he lies out on the barrens, he desperately longs for paternal love but can only find it missing.

Perhaps the story of the prodigal son is relevant here. As we all know, the story charts the journey of a son who leaves the father's home and squanders the father's resources, but who returns home and is welcomed back by the father. At first glance, the story of the prodigal son does not fit at all with the story of Hood. Hood's memories do not reveal a father who provided for the son, let the son go, and welcomed him back, but rather a father that, at least in Hood's recollection, abandons him at a tender developmental age. Yet the tenor of Hood's memories, despite the dark melancholic cloud hanging over them, might also reveal a longing for the welcoming father of the prodigal son story. As well, perhaps Hood's secret desire is for a more conventional interpretation of Job, one where reconciliation occurs after feelings of abandonment.

Hood now finds "his skeleton body sinking to this earth, bowed under the heavy, heavy memories that have always pulled him, he realizes now, down." (251) He sees now that "he was such a silly, gullible child, a child who thought he knew everything because he knew only the confident, simple world of English games, and endlessly elaborated, confident duty, words." (251) English games are instrumental in building the ego of English masculine character, a sense of control over the world. This is here extended in the duty of the English navy, which also provides the ego with a sense of mastery and control. But now the mastery and control of the ego is lost, and all that he is left with is trauma. And as he feels the "reassuring solidity of English steel against his hair" (251), he recalls the stanza from "Robbin-a-Bobbin" where the pigeon, the crow, the wren, and even the brother have been killed. Especially the line "and that will be all for gentle men." (252) Yet, Hood is "never able to complete ... the last syllable." (252) Gentle men do not stand a chance, especially gentle boys in the face of paternal abandonment. The last syllable floats in the air for Hood: "men ... men ... men."

Section

2

INTERSUBJECTIVE LOVE

1 RECOGNITION

The quest for gold is a central theme in *The Man from the Creeks*, since it tells a story about the Klondike Gold Rush by reworking, through narrative, the Robert Service poem "The Shooting of Dan McGrew." The quest for gold that drives the characters of Lou, Peek, Ben, Gussie, and Dan in Kroetsch's narrative is no simple quest for the jackpot of money. It is a quest for the ultimate object of desire, that which will completely fulfill desire. Yet, gold is not that ultimate object itself, for the object that completely fulfills only exists in the real, and thus is a non-object that can only be approximated through substitutes. Gold is, thus, to use Lacanian language, the *objet a*, an object of desire which stands as a substitute for the ultimate non-object of desire in the real.

It is in this sense that Kroetsch in his essay "Why I Went Up North" speaks of the quest for gold as quest for blankness and erasure. To go North and search for gold is to seek an unravelling of self in the hope that you are able to catch hold of the freedom acquired when you pass from the possession of gold to the real of desire.

Kroetsch thinks of this quest as a form of heroism, yet, when we turn to *The Man from the Creeks*, we soon realize that the distinctive heroism of the North that searches for the freedom of desire is intricately bound up with the search for love and home. This does not mesh with the common understanding that Kroetsch celebrates postmodern heroes that are bent on unravelling conventional definitions of self and desire. However, as Tiefensee has pointed out, Kroetsch's novels display a strong affinity for the kind of dialectical movements associated with Hegel; in fact, we have in Kroetsch not postmodern heroes, but Hegelian heroes. And it is significant that Hegelian heroes establish their heroism primarily through partnership.

In this first chapter of Section Two we will concentrate on the theme of recognition. Kroetsch's novel begins with the emerging form of recognition between Lou and Ben as they travel north to the Klondike. Drawing on the work of the psychoanalytic theorist Jessica Benjamin (1985), I will argue for an affirmative understanding of our identification with others and our dependency on their recognition. I will propose that, within the context of mutuality, identification and recognition can produce a negation where the other emerges as an outside other who can provide the subject with ideals of change that are transformative. I want to defend the connection of recognition and negativity and show how this connection is demonstrated in the ongoing relationship between Lou and Ben.

The first partnership established in *The Man from the Creeks* is that between mother and child, the bond between Lou and Peek. Lou and Peek are on a ship travelling north to Skagway. They are on their way to the Klondike to get rich on gold. It is Peek's birthday, and Lou decides to gives him a birthday gift, some cinnamon rolls stolen from the ship's kitchen. Lou's gift is a gift coming from the loving mother, an attempt by the mother to confirm and solidify the bond the son has with her. Yet, this is a bonding that quickly unravels in the face of the law, when Lou is caught as a thief.

The particular unravelling of this mother-son partnership in the face of the law is connected to issues of oedipalization. In the face of questioning by "some guy in a uniform" over the missing cinnamon rolls, Lou attempts to maintain the structural position of the father, even though the material father is absent. Peek whispers to her that he doesn't have a father. Lou responds: "Everyone has a father." (6)

In a sense, Lou and Peek, mother and son, form a dyad, yet Lou insists that they are part of a triad that includes the father as the third. If the presence of the third represents the law of society, then Lou's response to the uniformed man of the law is an attempt to normalize her and Peek's status.

Despite her attempts to invoke normality, Lou is accused of being a thief, of being contrary to the law. The stampeders on the ship are all gold-hungry. Lou, in her status as thief, becomes, in a sense, the cause of their desire. They do not know where the gold is; it is the missing object of their desire. Lou becomes the *objet a*, the spectral stand-in for the real, the shadow that blocks access to the object in the real. The stampeders shout at Lou in anger because her position as thief is bound up with her position as mother. The woman who loved and stole reminds them of the loved ones they left behind and reminds them of how broke they all are now. The stain at the heart of the real must be removed, must be sacrificed. So the stampeders intend to make Lou walk the gangplank.

Enter the stranger, Ben, whom we first encounter through his voice. Žižek has emphasized the notion of the traumatic voice, the voice whose presence is upsetting, which haunts the scene in such a way as to send us headlong into an encounter with the traumatic real itself. (1996) The stranger's voice is upsetting, but in a way that does not conform to Žižek's notion. His voice "didn't quite fit in with that crowd" (12), but the reason for the lack of fit is that, in comparison to the stampeders on the boat about to enact crude justice, the stranger was "listening as well as talking". (12) His was "a searching voice" one that was a "shade too gentle" for the mob. (12) He was a Klondiker, "but of a strange kind." (12)

The strangeness and the non-conformity of the stranger's voice come from its ground not in trauma, as Žižek would have it, but in intersubjectivity. The stranger Ben directs his presence toward recognition of the other, Lou, so that her legitimacy as a subject is confirmed, despite the attempts by the stampeders to deny it. I will have much more to say about intersubjectivity later, but at this point we can register an important theoretical dilemma: does strangeness and being ill-fit for the norm require the wrecking of normativity altogether and a traumatic passage into the void of the real, or does it require a doubling back to the norm, a passage through the norm toward freedom? The stranger Ben seems, at this point, to take the latter route, and does so through establishing a partnership with Lou.

The stranger's intervention, however, will require a payment. He says: "I'll pay this woman's fare." (12) Yet, when asked to produce the money payment, "the stranger offered his two empty hands." (13) He has no gold for payment of the debt owed by Lou's transgression. However, instead of gold, the stranger has whiskey to offer. All the other stampeders have carried with them the required grubstake to get them to the Klondike and to survive there materially as they sought their gold. The stranger, instead of a grubstake, has whiskey, and the stampeders are more than willing to wipe out Lou's debt in exchange for the sweet liquid. If Lou's transgression reminds them of their impoverishment, whiskey can surely make them feel rich again, if only momentarily. The "ecstasy" and "unspeakable bliss" (16) found in whiskey serves here as a seductive displacement for the object gold, which is itself a displacement for the ultimate non-object of desire. The stampeders have two barrels of whiskey, and Ben, Lou, and Peek are lowered in a boat to fend for themselves. They drift to the shoreline with their provisions.

It is soon discovered on the shore that Ben's grubstake contains none of the essentials of material survival, like flour and sugar that all Klondikers are supposed to have. Each Klondiker is required to have in his possession a year's supply of materials. However, Ben explains that all the boxes and sacks he has brought along are packed with sawdust and kegs of whiskey. The third has whiskey, not food. This brings to mind the basic distinction between need and desire. Need is immediately satisfied, like the mother's breast-milk for the child, like flour and sugar in the grubstake. Desire is always fulfilled (never fully, of course) through mediation. You need food to survive, but you desires whiskey, because it is whiskey that reminds you of the ultimate non-object. Whiskey reminds you of the real, not only because of the intoxication of the drink, but also because, and most perhaps more importantly, whiskey has a relationship with the more sought-after object of desire, gold. Whiskey as an object of desire works because you can trade with it. Ben explains to Lou and Peek that whiskey can be used as a trading item to get them to the gold that they want the most. One signifier of desire can be traded for another more important signifier of desire, in order to move closer the true cause of desire.

Lou's opinion of whiskey is related to her opinion of men and bars. Men frequent bars to drink whiskey and thereby forgo their role as fathers in the home. In other words, whiskey trades on male narcissism where the man removes himself from the partnership with the woman and the home to find an easy route to bliss through the bottle. Whiskey as an object of desire signifies for Lou a lack of partnership and a lack of recognition that comes through partnership. In her experience, whiskey has meant that the partner vacates the scene.

However, Ben disagrees with Lou's assessment of whiskey and seeks to convince her otherwise. He tells her that he has no intention of drinking the whiskey. He says to her, "We need it, partner." (29) Ben wants to be partners with Lou, and has no intention of leaving the scene. Lou knows of the advice that you don't get to the Klondike by yourself, but she is skeptical of Ben's advances. She asks Ben, "And what will this partnership cost me?" (30) She fears that the kind of partnership most men are interested in has nothing to do with mutuality but with finding a slave. Ben protests that he desires a mutual partnership and Lou finds her self drawn to his message: "she was listening." (31)

We can observe here the formation of a significant partnership that has as its third mediating element the presence of whiskey. A partnership with whiskey is to be distinguished from a lonely male with whiskey. They both seek a route to the cause of desire, but the partnership with whiskey establishes a triad that has as one of its distinguishing features a fundamental reliance on the intersubjective recognition of the partners. On the other hand, the lonely male with whiskey seeks to find desire outside its recognition of the concrete other, outside its relationship to this social ground. He wants to go straight to the source without mediation through the other, especially the feminine other.

On the shore, Lou and Ben, according to Peek, are "about to found a city." (36) They are hardly in a rush to get out of there. They first want to build a home. This home has whiskey as its ground. They "put together a snug-enough shelter." (43) It is even "homey." (43) And as they settle in, Ben and Lou begin to flirt. They do so by exchanging numbers about how the whiskey could be traded. Their desire for each other is enacted through an exchange relation. The whiskey brings them together. They can then sit around the fire, not drinking whiskey, but talking whiskey, a pure exchange relation. Ben and Lou together begin "calculating, guessing, journeying ... speculating." (44) These are all forms of mediated desire with whiskey the key third element and with home emerging as the ground.

Peek, who is narrating this story, tells us that he had been partners with Lou (even bed-partners on the boat), but that now his position is being usurped by Ben. In the new home on the shore, Ben and Lou put their quilts together to make one bed, with Peek now sleeping outside. Peek is not at all disturbed by this removal. In fact, he feels quite liberated now that he is no longer bound to a partnership of symbiosis with the mother. His desire is freed up to explore the exciting outside world while his mother Lou is preoccupied with her new partner. And he seems to be quite successful in a way, because he finds clams to eat, and a grizzly bear teaches him how to catch salmon (and isn't the grizzly here a unique kind of partner for Peek?).

————❖————

The search for gold by Ben and Lou and Peek is a richly symbolic one that indicates a distinctive relationship to the northern frontier, one that involves the experience of partnership, the relationship of one subject to the other. Jessica Benjamin, in her work *Like Subjects, Love Objects* (1985), asserts that although the subject may think it is self-constituting, it is invariably related to the other, first through identifications, and second through dependence of the recognition of the other. Only the second relationship can lead to what Benjamin calls intersubjectivity. Identification with the other can mean incorporating the other into the self and demanding, in a gesture of omnipotence, that the other be just like the self. Dependency on the recognition of the other can only occur through what Benjamin, using Hegelian terms, calls negation, where the other is an independent other who is able to act on the subject in such a way as to change the subject. (231) Thus there is a distinction to be made between "the other whom we create through our identifications and the concrete outside other." (233)

Recognition in relation to the negativity of the other is crucial because recognition can lead to a problematic "Hegelian synthesis" where the other is incorporated into the self and mastered. Identification then becomes a closed circuit of identity where the non-identical is excluded and we arrive at the problem of the imperious absolute subject. As Benjamin says, "if the other were not a problem for the subject, the subject would again be absolute." (233)

It is thus only when two concrete subjects enter into a partnership where each becomes a negative pole for the other that intersubjective recognition occurs. Is this what Ben and Lou are experiencing? Is this what Kroetsch is asserting about the quest for gold through their experience? Are they northern heroes in Kroetsch's sense? Remember Tiefensee's critique of Kroetsch. Her assertion is that the dialectical act of negation in Kroetsch's novels produces heroes who incorporate the other into the self, returning to a mastering identity that is unchanged by the experience. She is certainly correct to point out that this is a possibility within the structure of the Hegelian dialectic, a criticism I will return to later. Yet, she fails to mention the other possibility of dialectical unfolding, the other possibility of negativity, where the other is recognized in its otherness and fundamentally changes the structure of self, so that the return to self is a non-identical return. It is my belief that the partnership of Ben and Lou, and other partnerships we have yet to discuss (e.g., Peek and Gussie Meadows) are expressions of this second movement of the dialectic and negativity.

2 INTERSUBJECTIVITY

This chapter deals with the concept of intersubjectivity. The concept of intersubjectivity is closely tied to the workings of the dialectic. There are, however, different ways of interpreting the dialectic. Against the grain of Tiefensee's critique (1994, chapter 4) that Kroetsch's stories give us heroes whose dialectical struggles with otherness end up conquering and mastering otherness, I will argue that, in *The Man from the Creeks*, we are given heroes whose dialectical struggles with otherness do not conquer and master otherness, but reveal an inter-subjective ground of love.

The debate over the dialectic will involve a turn to interpretations of Hegel. I will first look at Žižek's fascinating Lacanian defense of Hegel (1989, 1993), where he sees the move from external reflection to determinate reflection as the production of an alienated image grounded in pure negativity, from which the subject reconciles himself with his lack.

Yet, whereas Žižek's Lacanian reading of Hegel denies the value of intersubjectivity, believing that the bonds of intersubjectivity are tied to imaginary forms of misrecognition, I want to argue for the value of intersubjectivity in understanding the nature of Hegelian heroes. We will trace the emergence in Hegel's *Logic* of an intersubjective structure, where the final movement of the "determinations of reflection" is established through the concept of "ground." This allows for a relation between conflicting determinations that define subjects and a commonality that lies beyond singular perspectives. We will refer to this relation and this commonality as one of "love," a love that does not cancel the difference of subjects but retains difference through the dynamics of intersubjectivity. Lastly, I will argue that Hegelian heroes generally, and the heroes in *The Man from the Creek* particularly, do not wish to close the gap between subjects through absolute knowing (Tiefensee and the critics of Hegel), nor are they seeking to work through negativity to the prime subjective awareness of lack (Žižek). Rather, they seek out partnerships of love that form the ground for the freedom of their desire.

On the trek up and through Chilkoot Pass, the stampeders are struck by an avalanche. Avalanches can wreak havoc on body and spirit, and this one determines very particular unravellings.

Although Ben, Lou, and Peek have for days been climbing "The Stairs" – like other stampeders, hauling their provisions on their backs, small load by small load – they miss being caught in the avalanche because Peek is sick. Peek has the shits. He's leaking big-time, unable to contain himself, unable to keep stuff locked inside. Yet, this leaking, this uncontainment, is itself contained within the tent-home that Ben and Lou have constructed at the bottom of the Pass. It's good to let it all out, cleanse the body and spirit of all the shit that has accumulated. But it's also good to feel safe in a space that holds you while you unravel, a space that contains the uncontaining.

The avalanche brings about another unravelling, different from Peek, but not unrelated. During the search for those caught in the avalanche, Lou comes back to the tent in a foul mood. She says to Peek, "They found your father." (101) The missing third that is nevertheless present seems here to be asserting its rights. Peek replies, "you never told me about *my* father." (102, emphasis in text) Lou asserts that "[e]verybody has a father." (102) The father who was always missing for Peek is now found, but the discovery reveals a dead father, a frozen phallus that is impotent yet important.

His importance for Peek lies in Peek's discovery that there are physical characteristics that he shares with his father – stringy brown hair, strong nose, bold ears. Yet, the story goes on to add that Peek's father, J Badger, shit when he died. Despite the imaginary lure of recognition provided by hair, nose, and ears, Peek discovers that big daddy phallus is just a piece of frozen shit.

Daddy as shit is intimately connected to Peek's shitting. At the same time as daddy phallus unravels to reveal itself as frozen and dead, Peek experiences an unravelling that is very much alive, one that burns through his ass. On the one hand, father is frozen and dead; on the other hand, son is running hot and alive. And it is significant that the alive unravelling of Peek – who is beginning to understand how useless and necessary the daddy phallus is – is contained within the tent-home, held by the presence of Lou and Ben. Two insights form here simultaneously: one, the necessary presence and subsequent realization of the frozen phallus, and two, the necessary presence and subsequent realization of the maternal container. The story reveals that both are required for the free flow of desire.

After making the final trek up Chilkoot Pass with their grubstake, Ben receives a letter from the customs agents that is written by a woman named Gussie Meadows. It reads: "Dangerous Dan is worried about my travelling alone. He says I should try to partner up with you." (113)

With reference to the debate between Derrida and Lacan about the status of the letter's arrival, Žižek (1992) claims that Derrida is wrong to criticize Lacan's contention that the letter always arrives at its destination. This is not a move into transcendental thinking, according to Žižek, because although the message always gets to where it's supposed to go, its arrival is marked by a fundamental incompleteness or lack that marks its connection to the real of desire. We could say that in the case of Gussie Meadows' letter, the letter arrives, but arrives incomplete, thereby setting in motion an unfolding of desire. Peek tells us that "It was Gussie Meadows who lured us on." (115) On to Lake Lindeman and Bennett City.

The letter arrives incomplete because we encounter very different interpretations as to the meaning of the message in the letter. And much of the conflict over interpretation has to do with the meaning of the "partnership" mentioned in the letter. Ben believes that it announces that Dan wants to get his "crowd" together in Dawson City in order to continue together, as a group, their quest for the gold. Ben's assumption is that there is a real intersubjective desire on Dan's part to bring everyone together to benefit equally in the riches of gold.

Lou interprets things much differently, and it is her interpretation that seems to foretell more of the story's subsequent unfolding, particularly in the way it is both right and wrong, or better, in the way it is right in being wrong. Contradicting Ben, Lou argues that the letter says nothing about getting a "crowd" together, only about Dan's intention of getting Gussie Meadows to Dawson City. Delivering Dan's possession, whom Lou calls a "namby-pamby fancy doll" (113), is the real meaning of Ben's "precious message." (115) The obvious implication here is of jealousy on Lou's part, jealousy for a woman referred to by the men as a "looker" entering into the intersubjective dynamics of the group to lure the desire, not only of Dan, but also possibly of Ben. Yet, as we shall see, the incompleteness of Gussie Meadows' letter and the desire for partnership is not so much about Dan in Dawson City, or even Ben, but instead concerns Peek, and specifically, Peek's sexual awakening.

Lou is right to see Gussie Meadows as a troubling element for the existing partnerships, but this trouble has less to do with her relationship with Ben (Lou thinking that Ben might chase after Gussie, ending their partnership), and more to do with the disturbance of the tie between mother and son. Lou's jealousy will turn out to have been significantly displaced, because her jealousy is for the partner who is a rival to the mother's love. This may not result in the death of her partnership with Peek, but may rather involve its displacement onto another scene, and its extension to wider networks of love and desire.

Different interpretations of the letter lead to differential unfoldings of partnership where love and desire are implicated. The letter arrives in such a way as to enact an interpretive play in which various partnerships, various intersubjective bonds, are released to the vagaries of love. Kroetsch's story of the search for gold is a story in which numerous partnerships of love unfold in a movement of the dialectic that establishes the identity of what we have called Hegelian heroes. Despite Dianne Tiefensee's suspicion (1994, chapter 4) that Kroetsch's stories bring us Hegelian heroes who triumph over difference and rule imperiously, there is in this story the emergence of partnerships of love in which difference and contingency are not sacrificed but celebrated within the context of bonding.

Tiefensee claims that Kroetsch's work indulges in a deconstruction of meaning in order to return to the source of desire. However, this deconstructive movement is, in her view, grounded in voice and presence. Voice has the power to attain presence through the telling of a story in which everything is undone and we arrive back at nothingness, the origin of desire. Tiefensee believes that this arrival back at the beginning ends up reconciling the divisions generated in the story so that we arrive once again at a non-divisive origin.

According to Tiefensee, the divisions in Kroetsch's stories are produced through a constant doubling, a doubling that invariably introduces a third element, and hence, produces a movement through triangulation. The presence of the triangle evokes the image of the dialectic. The dialectic works, as we all know, through negation. Tiefensee believes that in Kroetsch's stories the work of the dialectic serves to negate the self in order to return to the self. This, in fact, is the quest of the masculine hero. The hero pursues the full presence of self by positing the other as his own other and subsequently emerges heroic and victorious over the other.

Tiefensee contends that, rather than getting postmodern heroes in Kroetsch's works, we really end up with Hegelian heroes, men who use the drama of the story and the otherness available through the storytelling to conquer and master the other. Tiefensee's critique of Kroetsch sounds much like the critique of Savran concerning post–WWII American culture. To connect Tiefensee with Savran we can ask the following question: Is the masochistic logic in Kroetsch one that sacrifices the conventional masculine self in order to recapture a conquering masculinity associated with the oedipal father? In particular, is the story that unfolds in *The Man from the Creeks*, a story that charts a movement to the North, no different from the stories of the movement to the American western frontier, a story of the triumph of oedipal masculinity?

In order to better situate ourselves in this debate, especially as it concerns the workings of the dialectic, it may be helpful to turn to interpretations of Hegel's *Logic*. If Tiefensee is wrong about Kroetsch, perhaps she is wrong about Hegel as well.

One possible route to defending Hegel is through Žižek. In such works as *The Sublime Object of Ideology* (1989) and *Tarrying with the Negative* (1993), Žižek has argued that the vaunted self-reflection of Hegel consists in the continual failure of self-reflection, where self-consciousness confronts its own ungraspability, confronts the pathological stain that is the subject.

With reference to Hegel's *Logic*, Žižek maintains that "determinate reflection" is misunderstood. It is often believed (especially in left-Hegelian circles) that "determinate reflection" results in the elimination of alienation. Alienation is itself produced through the workings of "external reflection" where the essence is outside or opposed to the subject. This can be overcome, so it is thought (e.g., by Feuerbach), by the subject reappropriating the powers alienated in the other. Žižek finds this reappropriation problematic and contrary to Hegel's logic. According to Žižek's reading, we move from external to determinate reflection by experiencing the alienated image as the inverse of the essence as pure negativity. In other words, to use Lacanian language, the alienated image is established at the level of fantasy through the forms of the *objet a*, in response to which the subject does not attempt reconciliation through the means of a reflective mirror, but instead resolutely confronts its lack as a constitutive lack based in the real.

However, if we follow Žižek's reading of Hegel, the tensions arising from the relationship between the subject and other are never mediated by the presence of intersubjective bonds. There are no productive partnerships in Žižek. Peter Dews (1995), drawing on the work of Fink-Eittel, critiques Žižek for ignoring the emergence in Hegel's *Logic* of an intersubjective structure. Perhaps, then, Žižek is also wrong about Hegel.

If we turn to Hegel's *The Encylopaedia Logic* (1991), we can see the emergence of an intersubjective structure for thinking. Hegel argues that in "positing reflection" we only encounter the meanings we have projected on to things, generating a form of solipsism. In "external reflection" we experience helpless alienation by finding the meaning of the object outside our own being. It is in "determinate reflection" that we are able to establish a relation to an outside object which is "reflected into itself." How does this work?

If in "external reflection" we find that the meaning of the object is external to our subjectivity, "determinate reflection" overcomes the otherness of this insight by turning it into a "relating relation." It does so principally by understanding that the act of finding meaning is our own, our own ability to distinguish between a "surface" and an "interior." (§§ 115–120)

What then do we do with conflict over interpretation? For Hegel, the way to ensure that there is an awareness of the relation between conflicting interpretations is to draw attention to the final "determination of reflection" which is "ground." Ground highlights the commonality between conflicting interpretations despite their difference. (§ 121) The subject now grounds its identity through its relation to others, and begins to reflect and conceptualize from that ground. This does not mean the contingency of individual subjects is eliminated: it is as contingent, self-reflective individuals that subjects can affirm the commonality that binds them. In Dews' understanding, we can call this binding of subjects "love," a love that does not cancel the difference of subjects, but retains that difference through the dynamics of intersubjective recognition. (Dews: 244)

This brings us to Hegel's theory of the "concept." The concept overcomes the problem of abstraction, especially the problem of subjects abstracting from their relation to others. The subject now grounds its identity through its relation to others, and begins to reflect and conceptualize from that ground. And it is, in particular, the conceptuality of language, so fundamental to human social life that, as Dews tells us, "establishes a permanent possibility of reconciling conflicting subjective perspectives." (245) In this sense, the "life of the concept" refers to a "constant process of rupture and negotiation." (245) This does not mean the contingency of individual subjects is eliminated: it is precisely as contingent, self-reflective individuals that subjects come to accept and affirm the commonality that binds them." (245) Dews calls this "love," a love that does not cancel the difference of subjects, but retains that difference through the dynamics of intersubjective recognition.

There has been strong criticism of the Hegelian understanding of the concept. The suspicion has been that the tension between subject and other is reconciled in the perspective of absolute knowing where all negativity (and thus all the contingency and particularity of subjective life) is eliminated through the "negation of the negation." This critical suspicion is especially evident in the tradition of psychoanalysis. If the truth that psychoanalysis reveals to us involves the unpredictability and unmanageability of the real, then the promise of absolute knowing would be the denial of that truth. For Dews, however, the Hegelian "negation of the negation" involves something quite different from a difference-denying absolute, namely "the self-destruction of the negative relation between consciousnesses whose relation to themselves (and thus to each other) is negative or abstract ... with the result that the other ceases to be a limit to the self." (248) To negate the negative is thus to establish various partnerships of love, where subjects' relation to each other does not constitute a barrier to the unfolding of desire but its necessary condition, leading sometimes to unexpected arrivals.

Thus, Hegelian heroes do not attempt to eclipse the gap between self and other through absolute knowing (Tiefensee and the critics of Hegel), nor do they seek to pass, via negativity, into the abyss of the real (Žižek); rather, they seek out partnerships of love which, as ground, allow them the possibility for the freedom of desire. To see this unfold in Kroetsch's story we need to turn to the relationships that unfold in Bennett City.

Ben, Lou, and Peek arrive in Bennett City on the shore of Lake Bennett. Bennett City is a tent-city housing thousands of stampeders, all madly constructing boats, waiting for the ice to move out so that they can travel down the Yukon River to Dawson City. It is in Bennett City that Ben, Lou, and Peek find Gussie Meadows, who, they discover, has set up a hardware store to supply the stampeders with materials to build their boats.

Gussie Meadows' hardware store is not a brothel, even though Lou is convinced that it is. Lou may be right in a sense, for the story establishes strong associations between store and brothel, or more particularly, between work and desire. The store is not a brothel, yet there are lots of men coming out. As well, the colourlessness of the men is contrasted, first, with the many-coloured clothing of Gussie Meadows, colours that Peek associates with the colours of the rainbow, and, second, with the exotic smells the permeate the store, smells of roses, smells of the East.

While Ben and Lou establish a tent-home in Bennett City, and begin to plan the building of a boat, Peek is hired by Gussie Meadows to help out in the store. Peek knows how this all works, because of his work at his mother's store in Seattle (Lou ran a pawn shop there).

(124, 125) We see here the first indication of the strong connection, in Peek's experience, between Lou, his mother, and Gussie Meadows.

This connection is intensified when Ben and Lou enter the store and find Gussie Meadows feeding Peek. (127) Is she feeding him as generous boss, good mother, or as Peek's first lover? Peek and Gussie Meadows are talking and eating and laughing. (128) Clearly, the positions of boss, mother and lover are intermingling here. Lou is not impressed.

In the classic oedipal narrative for the boy, the father's position is one that, through identification (and possibly fear), draws the boy away from the clutches of the mother and introduces him to the exciting outside world of work and desire. This allows the boy (in the fixed heterosexual logic of the narrative) to then establish desire for other women, beyond the love of the mother. With Gussie Meadows we have the presence of the other woman, as rival to the mother. Yet, in Peek's case, there was no oedipal father to instigate this movement to the other woman. What is interesting about the position of Gussie Meadows is that she combines the role of paternal identification, maternal nurturance, and erotic lover. She is guide, boss, mother, and lover. To use Kristeva's terms (1982), we have here the presence of maternal-paternal conglomerate where desire is excited for Peek through a figure that is an extension of the mother's love, yet at the very same time, takes on the role of paternal guide in the world of work. We therefore have, in Gussie Meadows, the presence of the "imaginary father."

Gussie Meadows becomes an imaginary figure of identification for Peek where a distinctive intermingling of work and desire are manifested. While busy in the aisles of the hardware store, Peek and Gussie are constantly bumping into each other, which gets Peek's juices going. At night he masturbates buried in his bearskin blanket and fantasizes being buried in Gussie's skirt. (132) Both the bear and Gussie bear the mark of a third for Peek, but a particular third that both partakes in the maternal connection and seeks distance from it.

The Bear has been a constant presence for Peek on this journey. While on the shore, with Ben and Lou busy doing the home thing, Peek goes off looking for adventure and food. He encounters a grizzly bear who teaches him how to catch fish with his bare hands. The bear thus becomes a kind of paternal guide, teaching lessons in the outside world of labour. Later at the summit of Chilkoot Pass, the trappers provide Peek with a bearskin blanket to keep warm. Ben and Lou decide to buy this blanket as a present for Peek. Here, added to the role of paternal guide, we have maternal container. Yet, it is a maternal container that is removed or distanced from the embrace of his mother, and this distance allows him to masturbate and dream of Gussie.

Lou, as a jealous mother who mistakes the son's lover for a whore, thinks Peek should leave the hardware store, afraid he is being corrupted by the bad outside world. Gussie intervenes, now in the role of businesswoman, and says that Peek can't leave. He's needed as a worker, the paternal guide announcing to the mother that her son is now needed in the outside world of work and desire.

One day after work, Peek stays with Gussie Meadows for supper. They move into Gussie's private place at the back of the store. What is interesting about Peek's experience here is the near-total lack of mastery he enjoys in the presence of Gussie. If the phallus is presumed to master, and if Peek's entry into the exciting outside world of desire is meant to initiate that mastery, then here we find that the phallus fails both miserably and pleasurably.

Upon entering her private place, Peek catches the scent of pure ambrosia and it makes him dizzy. Peek asks Gussie about Dan McGrew, who he thinks is her true lover, the true bearer of the absent phallus. Gussie replies that "I'm here and he's there." (139) Yet, Peek is also here and he is holding hands with Gussie.

As Gussie calls Peek a "man" and asks him, "Have you ever kissed a woman?" (140) Peek replies that he has "kissed Lou." (140) Gussie finds that a strange answer. Perhaps she is not aware of the extent to which she has become a maternal extension. Gussie proceeds to kiss him and Peek tries to return the kiss. She likes it that he doesn't know how to kiss, enjoys the mentorship.

Peek then buries his face in Gussie's slip, just as he had done earlier in fantasy. Gussie's stockings, made of silk, smell of basil and cinnamon, again making Peek dizzy. These erotic, dizzying smells in Gussie's private place remind Peek of the smells of the apartment he and Lou had in Seattle. Gussie pulls her skirt over Peek's head and he is instantly sent into a topsy-turvy pleasurable confusion. It is significant that Peek, in learning to be a man, approaches Gussie, not with phallic mastery, but with a dizzying confusion of the senses. Peek's manly training brings a non-mastery (unmanly in the traditional sense) that sends him beyond ego-pleasure, into a different form of pleasure, a pleasure that speaks to a distinctive form of the death-drive, the death of control and mastery.

Things are even more scrambled when we try to make sense of Gussie's position here. In the traditionally conceived arrangement, it is important not to mix identification with desire. In the case of the boy's maturation, the boy's desire for the mother is interrupted by the identification with the father, who allows him to transfer his desire from mommy to a future mate. The paternal figure of identification, for the boy, is not to be mixed with the feminine figure of desire. This allows the boy to assume a sense of mastery over the id through identification with the father that can then be applied to the outside figure of desire, who is a substitute for the mother.

However, when we look at Peek's relationship with Gussie, we see that she serves as a figure of identification, assuming the position of the traditional third, allowing him separation from his mother Lou. His identification is with both a feminine and a masculine third. On the one hand Gussie is a feminine third, who indulges in the exotic colours and smells of the feminine, and who offers a dizzying space of confusion for Peek's desire that leaves him in a position of pleasurable non-mastery. On the other hand, she is a masculine third, teaching Peek how to handle a gun and how to shoot accurately. As Peek tells us, "She was showing me ... how to build a space around myself." (146) Thus, we have confusion of boundaries at the same time as building of boundaries.

This issue of masculine and feminine identification is explored in an important essay by Jessica Benjamin entitled "Sameness and Difference" (1985). Benjamin begins by stating that our understanding of sexual difference is "no longer seen as being triggered by the discovery of anatomical facts." (49) In light of this, she wishes to explore now the ways in which the body comes to *figure* difference. Despite this understanding, the dominant assumption in the culture at large is that acknowledging the difference between males and females has a higher value than recognizing the sameness between them. How might we incorporate difference without repudiating sameness? Possibly we could establish a tension rather than a strict opposition. (50)

Benjamin wants to look critically at the notion of identity. For sexual identity has come to mean a fixed difference with strong boundaries between masculine and feminine. She believes we need some framework that embodies plurality. We need to make a distinction between identity as rigid and identification as more plural. This leads her to formulate a conception of sexual difference that moves away from the rigidity of the oedipal model, one that incorporates the many identifications that exceed the rigidities of identity prescribed by the oedipal model. (52)

What has been previously undervalued is the "coming together of likeness and difference." (53) Especially identification with the parent of the opposite sex. Here we have an identification that crosses the boundaries set up by identity as rigid sexual difference. Benjamin tells us that both girls and boys are originally bisexual in that they identify with both parents. They are "overinclusive" in that "they believe that they can have or be anything." (53)

Although boys and girls may begin with a nominal gender identification, this is not a core gender identity. The self identifies being part of one gender through "concrete representations of self-body and self-other body interactions, which are retroactively defined as gendered." (54) Yet, this identification is very tenuous. The child still identifies with both parents, who are only beginning to be differentiated from each other. In fact, this core sense of belonging to one sex does not organize all experience of gender. It only makes sense if we think of it as the starting-point from which future gender ambiguity arises. (55)

According to Benjamin, the nominal gender identification is succeeded by an early differentiation of identifications in the context of separation-individuation. Traditionally, the father represents separation, agency and desire, and even if this holds, ideally, both boys and girls continue to identify with both parents so that the father is important for the girl as well as the boy. Benjamin calls this parental figure of identification the rapprochement father. Yet, she is emphatic that this figure can be played by figures other than the biological father who represent separate subjectivity. (57)

The above considerations mean that an important distinction must be made between the rapprochement father and the classic oedipal father, a distinction similar to the one Kristeva makes between the imaginary father and the oedipal father. The function of the rapprochement father, whether male or female, is to enter into a dyadic relationship with the child. This is distinct from the triadic function of the oedipal father who forbids access to the mother. The rapprochement father embodies the desire for the outside world without foreclosing the bonds of attachment associated with the mother. (57) Benjamin is pointing to the importance of a second adult in the child's life with whom he can identify. The importance is not tied to the person forbidding access to the mother and sending the child out into the world, but in creating a "second vector" which points outward.

This is the role that Gussie plays in Peek's development. She is a "second vector" that allows his desire to point outward away from his mother but without repudiating his mother, especially his mother's love. Peek constantly insists on love. He questions Gussie continually as to whether she loves Dan McGrew. Despite Gussie's own disillusionment with romantic love, Peek reveals a persistent idealism that charms Gussie, and excites her identification within which she serves as mentor and guide.

Yet, is not the love that identification spurs hopelessly romantic? Benjamin believes that we may have to revise our conception of identificatory love. In traditional psychoanalytic theory, identificatory love is associated with idealization. It is viewed as a defensive function where loss of control over the mother is overcome through idealization of the figure of identification. It is a way of sustaining the narcissism that would otherwise be challenged. (58)

Although this may in some cases be true, the idealization of identificatory love is not only defensive, but represents symbolically all those ideal aspirations of the child for activity in the exciting outside world. Benjamin contends that this perspective on identificatory love is contrary to the Lacanian perspective where the subject in love becomes trapped and alienated in an imaginary idealized image, where the subject is literally "subjected" to the image of the loved one. In contrast to this Lacanian perspective, Benjamin claims that "the acts of creating the ideal, forming an identificatory bond, and actively pursuing the relationship with the beloved figure, are, in effect, the subject's own." (59) It is the active casting outward that forms desire, one that can potentially move from figure to figure, and thus is not trapped in one figure and one relationship.

In the case of Peek, if the above holds, then Gussie's function for Peek is not to initiate a radical separation from maternal love. She is not a traditional oedipal third that requires the boy to leave behind the idealism associated with the maternal connection. In fact, the idealism associated with the maternal connection is now transferred, through Peek's own active desire, from its original association with the maternal container – Peek in relation to Lou – to the exciting outside world of love associated with Gussie.

3 THE CONTRACT

This last chapter in Section Two explores the concept of the contract. In attempting to make sense of the contract between Ben and Dan on digging for gold and how that contrasts with the partnership established between Ben and Lou, I will turn once again to the work of Hegel and his understanding of the contract in the *Philosophy of Right* (1981).

I will argue along with Hegel that, ideally, we can establish the contract on an intersubjective rather than individualistic ground. I will maintain, along with Michael Theunissen (1991), that if we ground the contract in intersubjectivity we arrive at an expression of communal love that gives us access to a living good and a taste of universal life. The fundamental movement in intersubjectivity, I will argue, is the movement from "mine-ness" to "own-ness" where my accomplishments are sublated in their immediacy, and thus shorn of their solipsism, by being presented in external form in the communal contract, where others see themselves through those accomplishments.

My contention will be that Ben's understanding of the contract occurs through the structure of own-ness and that this understanding conflicts with Dan's, which occurs through the structure of mine-ness. This sets up the fateful showdown in the Malamute Saloon between Ben and Dan and the final episode in the "Shooting of Dan McGrew."

———————

Having arrived in Dawson City, Ben, Lou, and Peek can see the men heading out to the creeks. Some of them can hardly walk. Peek notes a kind of embarrassment in their walk, despite their attempt to swagger. These men have stumbled into the saloon for one last drink before they head out to get rich. They chase after the gold, but that chase too often is displaced by the glass of whiskey, whiskey that is watered down. Instead of gold, there is whiskey. Instead of a confident swagger, there is an embarrassing stumble. (195)

In the Malamute Saloon, three gallons of whiskey sit beside a pair of gold scales. These scales are made of solid brass and look to Peek like "some kind of crazy huge golden butterfly." (197) A beauti-ful butterfly, no doubt, but the perception is ambivalent, because Peek also sees a fierce insect, poised and polished, about to "at any second leap, or lunge, or take flight, or attack you head on, or even make some kind of awful mating sound." (197) The scales are thus both ideal and monstrous at the same time, polished and shining, charming to the gaze, but also a creature about to devour you. This is the measure of gold for the stampeders seeking to get rich. They chase after an impossible creature, "some kind of insect" (197) that is strange, out of this world. This is not an unpleasurable experience. The pleasure that comes from the measure of gold is one that speaks to the demands of the death drive, a pleasure beyond the pleasure principle ruled by ego-constancy.

Dan McGrew enters and so does his piano. This is the first meeting between Dan and Ben, Lou, and Peek. Peek describes Dan as a handsome man with an unnaturally pale face. Dan's paleness could be related to his time spent much earlier in the States hiding in a barrel from gamblers trying to collect a debt. That's how Ben knew Dan, because Ben had risked his life to save him. Dan hid in the barrel in a fetal position, completely in the dark. His infant-like experience has as its complement his present demeanor as the owner of the saloon. Peek tells us that Dan "had a big-man way about him." (200) This swagger is belied however by the fact that while the stampeders trek out to the creeks to dirty themselves, Dan stays hidden in the saloon, with polished boots that have no dirt on them. Despite his masquerade of power, Dan is still in the barrel, still locked in infancy. The image of the powerful phallus that marks the outward presence of Dan's masculinity is quickly punctured by Dan's lack.

The saloon is surely an advance over the barrel. It is not so tight or so constricting for activity. Its displacing power is directed toward its status as container-home, and container-homes are necessary grounds for the activity of the subject. In Dan's case, however, there is the lurking suspicion that the saloon as container is fundamentally marked by the demands of the infant to be pleased without returning the pleasure, without recognizing the demands of the other subject.

This is confirmed and made more complex by the arrival of the piano. Dan has bought a piano for the saloon so that Gussie Meadows can dance to it. Yet, he can't seem to give the workers the proper instructions to get the piano down from the wagon. Lou rescues Dan and gives instructions to the men, giving advice that sounds like an order. Dan's inability to give instructions might be due to the fact that his mind is wandering, in a dream-like state. He is waiting for Gussie Meadows. Waiting rather than acting has taken hold of Dan, and Peek observes that he is "the kind of man who stood there expecting to be greeted and embraced and coddled." (203)

This inactive waiting unsettles Ben. Ben remembers that he and Dan had communicated while Dan was hiding in the barrel and that a set of promises had been made at that time. Dan had proposed a partnership concerning a stake in the creeks. Ben expected that when he finally arrived in Dawson City, and he and Dan met face-to-face, this partnership would be consolidated, and what he believed to be an intersubjective agreement between two individuals who recognize each other would be confirmed. Yet, nothing happens. Dan does not communicate with Ben and will not confirm the partnership. He will not return the recognition, and Ben is left waiting. (203)

All the talk is about Gussie Meadows. Dan wants to know if they were able to hook up with Gussie and escort her to Dawson City. Ben explains that she isn't with them, that she decided to return home with her gold. At this point, Dan's face turns from pale to dark, and he turns his back on Ben. (204) Dan's sudden melancholic mood fits with the state of infancy that hides behind his big-man demeanor. He hides in the saloon waiting for his love object to arrive. And even though the saloon appears to be an advance over the barrel in that Dan is making a load of money off the stampeders with his watered-down whiskey and his scales, he expects that this should confirm his relationship with Gussie. He has the money-making saloon to provide for her, and now he has the piano to show her off in all her colours. However, Gussie had set up her own shop, and had made her own money, and decided not to be the showpiece for Dan. She abandons him, turning Dan all dark. Deprived of the one-way recognition from Gussie (he would be the subject, she would be the object), his mirage of confidence suddenly turns to the pouting of the infant.

Peek takes a special pleasure in Dan's melancholy. He hands Dan a message from Gussie that says, "I'm going back to Frisco, Dan. Just as well. I was coming there to kill you." (207) As we have already witnessed, the letter always arrives and the message here that announces the presence of the death drive must be fulfilled. The only question is: In what particular fashion will the death drive unfold, and how will its attendant pleasures be expressed?

The piano is significant in this unfolding and this expression. After Dan finally decides on its placement, both Ben and Peek play. Peek learned how to play in his mother's pawnshop, and now he plays for Dan while Dan reads the letter from Gussie. Really, he plays for Gussie, using the rivalry with Dan to spur on his powers of concentration. He used to play for Lou, his mother, but now he plays for Gussie, his displaced maternal love object. However, at this point, the love for Gussie is mediated by the rivalry with Dan. In effect, the pleasure taken in the death-like downfall of Dan, the rivalrous third, is sublimated into a vigorous and concentrated playing. Somebody in the saloon observes, "Hey, that kid's pretty good." (209)

Dan's response to the letter is unexpected. Peek expects Dan to be dangerous but instead he is generous. He offers Ben, Lou, and Peek the cabin he had built for Gussie. Yet this generosity has a peculiar tone to it. Peek observes that "it was as if the voice that spoke out of his mouth wasn't his to order around." (210) It's almost as if the message of the letter has taken over Dan's subjectivity, speaking for him. The voice, as Žižek (1995) reminds us, can often be a traumatic voice, haunting the scene. There is a death-like spectre that emanates from Dan's voice, conveying a ghostly image. Faced with being abandoned by Gussie, Dan concentrates even more on getting the gold, the *objet a* that might suture the wound that gapes, the lack coming from the real. The offer of the home for Lou, Ben, and Peek is only a means to that end. Ben must go to the creeks to find the gold, and in the meantime Lou and Peek need a home.

This offers a distinctive perspective on home. Dan has no interest in building a home that might serve as a secure maternal-like container for his desire. He skips all mediating structures in the belief that he can obtain the object that will relieve him of the anxiety associated with lack and allow him direct access to the fulfilled desire. Dan has no use for the mother, or for the father's mediating role in relation to the mother.

The contrast with Ben is striking. Ben also plays the piano once it is placed in the saloon. Lou says to him that he never told her that he played the piano. Ben's reply is that his mother made him play, which implies to Peek that his mother pushed him around. Lou is especially intrigued by the introduction of Ben's mother. She asks him if he cared for his mother. An impossible question, thinks Peek, but one that "offered a little lesson in love and responsibility." (213) Dan brought the piano in for Gussie, who he hoped would patch up the hole in his desire. For Ben, and for Peek as well, the piano has something to do with love and responsibility, those conditions associated with mother and home.

Ben mentions that his mother has been very sick for quite some time, that, in fact, he has had to take care of her since he was thirteen, due to the trauma of his father's death. His father died in a train accident. It was, says Ben, "[t]he steam…. He was boiled alive." (214) Peek replies, "Like the opposite of an avalanche." (214) Peek's father had died in the avalanche at the Pass, and the connection to the death of Ben's father is clear to him. Both Ben and Peek are strongly tied to their mothers, and both are in some way trying to replace their fathers in the home, taking on the paternal task of love and responsibility. While in Dan's case, death represents a haunting presence that threatens to send him headlong into the abyss of the real, in Ben and Peek's case death, in particular, paternal death, represents a task of love, to build homes and take care of their mothers. When Lou asks Ben if he misses his mother, Ben replies, "I'll be back there before too long. I hope." (214) Ben's desire for the gold is a desire to return home, to return in fulfillment to the mother.

In a sense, Ben seeks a return to the self through the acquisition of gold. It seems quite clear at this point that this does not conform to Žižek's interpretation of a Hegelian return. That is, Ben's return is not one who passes through the failure of paternal love in order to arrive at the void of the real. Rather, Ben's return is to home, to the love of the home. However, it is also clear that Ben's return is not an abandonment of paternal love in favour of an exclusive embracing of maternal love. Instead, Ben pursues a unique form of paternal love, one that exists in solidarity with maternal love.

Ben, Lou, and Peek arrive at the cabin Dan has allowed them to use, and they are impressed by its newness, its new logs, new windows, new paint, and new fence. (217) They fall in love with the place and dream of making it their home, just like the rudimentary homes they had built on the shore, in Skagway, at Dyee, and in Bennett City. (218) Dan is waiting for them there, and he is not at all interested in the fashioning of a home. He wants to talk about a partnership with Ben in order to find gold, a partnership defined by a very distinctive form of contract.

Ben tells Dan that he is three thousand dollars short on the amount of money he had promised to bring to the deal. Dan replies that this is bad news, that now Ben will really have to work. In Dan's mind, work constitutes a severe punishment, for Dan's approach to acquiring money is to work as little as possible directly in the material world. Dan is a gambler, and money for him is pure exchange value. To the extent that money depends on material labour, Dan expects others to perform the dirty work, the work in the dirt.

Ben has a different approach. He says, "I'm no stranger to work." (221) Back in Iowa he loved his work as a cooper making the whiskey barrels. He loved pounding on the barrels to shape them properly. To Dan, however, the sound of pounding was deafening, because he was hiding from a gambling debt in a barrel. Ben says he took great pleasure in firing the old cask, whereas for Dan the smoke produced by the firing was suffocating. In the barrel, not working, Dan plays the part of the infant for whom the sounds and smells of the outside world of work are disturbing. There seems to be an intimate relationship between Dan as gambler and Dan as infant in the barrel. Both gambling and infancy avoid the labour of work, hoping for the instant payoff, instant gratification that comes from the labour of others. It is in this sense that Dan seeks to enter the partnership with Ben as master to slave, expecting Ben (like the mother) to perform the material labour that will bring him his fortune.

Dan tells Ben that he has obtained, through gambling, a small claim up on Eldorado Creek. He proposes a partnership with Ben through a contract. Ben will do the work, the mining, and when he finds the gold, they will split the profits 50/50. Ben accepts the offer and is told by Dan that he must leave right away, in order to hasten the acquisition of gold.

What is the nature of the partnership through a contract that Ben has with Dan and how does it differ from the partnerships Ben has been developing with Lou and Peek? To answer this properly, I want to propose an interpretation of Hegel's understanding of the contract in *The Philosophy of Right* (1981). My interpretation has been aided by a wonderful essay by Michael Theunissen on the concepts of contract and intersubjectivity in Hegel (1991).

Hegel's *Philosophy of Right* attempts to articulate a freedom for which the other is not an obstacle but the path through which freedom is realized. The important question that arises in Hegel's analysis of the foundations of civil society is whether freedom is based in the individual or mediated intersubjectively.

The attempt to ground freedom rests on a consideration of ethical life. For Hegel, any treatment of ethical life must begin with the family, in particular, the civil family. The family is the most basic form of unity in society, a unity that is communal in character and is expressed through love. (§ 158) We encounter here a freedom of the loving community, which is determinate and concrete, but at the same time commits individuals to a universal life through the claims of intersubjectivity. (§ 181) If the partnerships generated between Ben, Lou, and Peek (as well as Gussie) are, as I have argued, intersubjectively based, then, in Hegel's terms, those partnerships are expressions of communal love that bring each of them freedom through their access to a universal life, a universal life that goes beyond the constraints of solipsistic (and thus non-social) individuality.

Hegel has often been criticized for uncritically endorsing existing forms of communal life and familial life as expressions of universal freedom. However, there is a critical attitude that emerges in the *Philosophy of Right*, and that involves the conception of "life." (§ 70) Against the abstract idea of the good, Hegel emphasizes the living good whose concealed intersubjectivity finally reveals itself as "universal life."

The commitment to the living good that is grounded in intersubjectivity brings forward a critique of the contract and private property as the bases for civil society. Here's where the contrast between Ben and Dan comes in. If Ben's partnerships with Lou and Peek are intersubjectively based, they can be viewed as critically opposed to Dan's proposal of a partnership based on the contract and the acquisition of private property.

The ground for freedom in Hegel is the relation of will to will. (§ 71) This is an essential relation because of the reciprocity implicit in the contract. The contract is an exchange contract where my property is recognized by others. Yet, a fundamental tension quickly arises. In the contract, I am involved with others. At the same time, though, if I assert my right to property and let the other individual have his own, I end up without a relation to the other individual and am indifferent to him. (§ 72) This indifferent relation of partners to the contract affects the consciousness of the subjects who enter the contract, resulting in a consciousness of fundamental non-involvement.

The lack of relatedness stems from the nature of property as such. Hegel conceives of property as both individualistic and solipsistic. An owner of property is someone alone in the world. The contract based on property strips individuals of their sociality. In this sense, the individual owners of property exhibit a form of social deficiency where a positive relation to the will of other individuals is absent.

Isn't this the kind of contract that Dan envisages for the mining of gold on Eldorado Creek? Because Dan has no interest in the bonds of intersubjectivity, because he has no desire for home, his 50/50 proposal effects a relation of indifference, not the sociality of community. As in the barrel, Dan remains in a poor, isolated, solipsistic world that requires him to be the master who profits from the labour of the slave, and thus deprives him of the subjective recognition from the other which he nevertheless so intensely craves. But Dan is a gambler and his craving for recognition comes through the all-or-nothing framework: either I win it all (as in the demands of the infant for the all of the mother's gaze) or I have nothing.

Perhaps, though, Ben's acceptance of the 50/50 contract belies a different orientation. For Hegel in the *Philosophy of Right*, intersubjectivity is achieved through an identity in the exchange contract that proceeds through purchase and sale. In the purchase and sale relationship, where there is a flow of giving and receiving, a contradiction emerges for the subject through the alienation of property. I give up myself as a non-involved and indifferent property owner when I consciously integrate myself into the community of other property owners. This allows me to be one among others at the same time as just myself, a contradictory structure of "is and is not." (§ 73) However, in order for this to work, I must have the orientation to my own subjectivity that allows my subjectivity to be exchangeable. I can easily exchange things because I know myself to be exchangeable with others, and thus, in a fundamental sense, indiscernible from others. (§ 77)

This establishes, for Hegel, the universality of identical wills who are now abstract persons in civil society. The criticism of Hegel has been that this universality and abstraction of the individual comes to subsume the particular individual, thus subsuming individual freedom under the more abstract freedom of the state. Although this absorption of the individual in the universal is certainly present in the *Philosophy of Right*, there is also another current of thought in Hegel's text that points in a different direction. This is particularly true in the movement from property considered "mine" (where there is a severely limited notion of commonality, which cannot free itself from its source in the egoism of private property) to an intersubjective awareness that is able to hold in place the tension between individuality and universality. My accomplishments are my accomplishments only insofar as I am able to sublate their immediacy in having them present to me in an external form. This externality is present to others, and others begin to look at themselves in my accomplishments. In this way, my accomplishment is linked to the will of others, where I am, as an accomplishing agent, the other I am for others. (§ 112)

Ben has consistently viewed his accomplishments from the perspective of own-ness or intersubjectivity. He has laboured hard to fashion wood into barrels, and his accomplishment is reflected in the barrels of whiskey he hauls on board the ship to Skagway. Yet, his desire was always to give that possession up to the other. First, he seeks Klondike fortune only to return to Iowa to properly take care of his invalid mother. Then, he gives up his possession in order to pay Lou's debt on the boat, and soon desires to establish a familial and communal bond with both Lou and Peek. Within that bonding, the possession of whiskey becomes the lubricant for a series of exchange relations, the three of them forming a community of love based on intersubjective recognition.

Ben wishes to continue that project in submitting himself to the work of mining for gold. His externalized accomplishment there only makes sense through his desire for home, his hoped-for return to the maternal home in Iowa, and his continuing establishment of a home with Lou and Peek, now at the cabin in Dawson City.

My argument has been that Ben desires love, and in desiring love desires home. Yet, as we have seen, it is impossible, when considering Ben's experience, to think about home without, at the same time, thinking about work. Ben has a distinctive relation to work that is highlighted in his digging for gold at Dan's claim.

Dan is pressuring Ben to get right to work. He wants Ben to go fast. This in keeping with Dan's desire to obtain the object of desire quickly, the instantaneous arrival of satisfaction. Peek comments that Ben is not like that. Ben does not move fast. No quick in and out for Ben. He has staying power. He sticks to the job. This speaks to the question of the mediation of work. Dan gambles to go straight to the real of satisfaction, wishing to bypass the mediating activity of labour. He wants to go straight from the barrel-womb to the encompassing and enveloping experience of the real.

At first glance, it might seem that Dan embodies the characteristics of active masculinity. He has a big-man way about him that suggests an assertive confidence. It also seems that Dan is the active agent in the world of business and commerce. He owns the saloon, and also owns the claim on Eldorado Creek that he hopes will yield gold. In short, Dan is the man of capital, and parades about with the forceful aggressiveness so often associated with the successful capitalist.

However, this masquerade of confidence is belied by an anxiety that runs deep. Dan's subjectivity is consumed with the experience of the barrel, and in this way marks a man severely limited and confined in his ability to access the outside world of objects. Like Hegel's master, Dan depends on the work of the other, the slave, to provide that access. In his relationship with Ben, this began in the barrel, when Ben took care of him and allowed him his escape from his pursuers. Now, that relation of dependence continues with Ben heading to the claim to perform the labour of digging for gold. The master wants the gold straight away, while the slave has access to the gold through the mediation of labour.

The reversal goes further. As Judith Butler comments (1997: 39–41), the master might look like he has access to difference because he is able to enjoy the fruits of the slave's labour. In this sense, Dan as master-capitalist is the ultimate consumer, because he is able to devour what others under his command produce, leaving nothing of permanence behind. This seems to provide Dan with an experience of the transitory state of desire, which can be contrasted with Ben's experience of labour, because Ben slaves away on the material object, providing for him a kind of permanence to desire.

This is illusory, however, because Ben as slave-labourer experiences a unique form of loss in relation to the material object. In his labour, Ben is always giving up himself and the object to others. Ben feels an obligation to provide for his ailing mother. And now he has developed bonds of attachment where his desire is to give himself up in his labour to provide for Lou and Peek. Although Ben displays characteristics of permanence – staying power, sticking to the job – this permanence is linked to a fundamental relationship to lack and loss, the lack and loss of ego.

Thus, Ben's quest for gold is entirely distinct from Dan's. Dan wants unmediated access to the object which will patch up the hole in his desire. What appears as a confident encounter with lack turns out to be an attempt to bypass lack altogether. Ben, in contrast, thrives on mediation. His quest for gold is oriented toward labour on the material object, and because of that labour, he settles in with lack through the structures of work and home.

Peek's relationship with Ben runs entirely on this trajectory, a trajectory that involves the mediation of home and work. Peek has a plan. He decides to go check on Ben out in the mines. His first encounter with the men at work in the mines hardly brings to mind traditional images of heroism. Peek comments that the men "moved around me like scorched old trees that had learned to walk." (231) It looks to Peek like there are thousands of men here who have lost their minds, piling up mounds of muck only to find, after they have run water through the rockers, minimal traces of gold.

At Eldorado Creek, Peek finds Ben "sitting dead still." (233) Peek asks him where the mine is that he is working on. Ben points to a miserable-looking hole, and explains that they are not deep enough yet. As Peek goes on ranting and raving about good luck and fortune, Ben returns to his hole, to his slave work. In contrast to Dan's child-like passivity in the barrel, his non-work, Ben's hole is one of constant, filthy toil with little prospect of gain. Peek observes that Ben looks too old to be digging in the permafrost, like those pictures of elderly coal miners, with their beaten faces and broken-down bodies, still putting in the time to pay the rent. While Dan sits comfortably at the gambling table in the Malamute Saloon, Ben sleeps with his mud-caked clothes on in a dirty, filthy ramshackle cabin. And Peek joins him, at least for a while, painstakingly tunnelling through the bedrock, with Ben digging and Peek hauling.

After fourteen days of digging, Ben and Peek decide to pay Lou a visit. Lou is now working for Dan at the Saloon, weighing the gold brought in by the miners. Ben and Peek find her all done up with feathers and colours, in sharp contrast to their own filthiness. In a certain sense, Lou is now aligned with Dan. She is clean and all spruced up because she doesn't need to enter the hole of dirty mine labour; her living, like Dan's, is dependent on the miners bringing in their claims and then drinking and gambling away their profits. Lou finds that she can talk to Dan. She believes that they share some common bond because both of them have been in hiding. Hiding "marks you for the rest of your life." (254) It "fills you up with secrets." (254) The common bond of hiding shared with Dan affects her perception: although pleased to see Ben and Peek, she says they are a sight for sore eyesthey are in desperate need of new clothes. When Ben and Peek ask Lou if she will join them out at the claim, her response is not at all positive. She doesn't think much of the prospects out in the mines; in fact, not hearing from Ben led her to think that maybe he "fell into a hole. Disappeared." (243) She prefers hiding in the saloon to the disappearance in the hole of filth and dirt. Perhaps the secrets she and Dan are hiding by displaying strong master-egos in the saloon are not so easily concealed if their egos disappear in the slave-labour of the dirty hole. The cleanliness of the barrel-womb is to be preferred to the shitty hole.

Yet, in another sense, Lou is more like Gussie Meadows, using Dan's invitation (to work at the Saloon, to live in the cabin) to profit from the mad attempt by stampeders to strike it rich. Dan and Lou are partners, for now, but Lou has no desire, like Gussie, to get trapped in Dan's infantile barrel. Lou wants to make money to secure a home, either here or elsewhere, with Ben and Peek. And she realizes quite quickly that Dan squanders money just as fast as he makes it, that while she toils fourteen hours a day running the saloon, Dan is in his gambling corner wiping away the profits. So, when Dan offers Lou a 50/50 deal on the saloon, proposing, in effect, that they become partners, Lou replies, "That will be one goddamned frosty Friday in hell." (251) Meanwhile, Ben has quietly travelled back to the mine.

In the middle of December, Lou decides to do up a roast and take it to Ben at Eldorado Creek. Peek tags along. Lou and Peek find the hole Ben is working on and descend down the shaft. When they find Ben drifting he hardly acknowledges them and says he wants to finish what he is doing. Peek desperately wants Ben to find gold, so that "the dark would glow yellow." (272) Why are both Peek and Ben so desperate for the gold? Ben has worked hard in the mines, slaved away at the claim, and Peek wants to join him in the labour, wants to become a slave for gold as well. Ben, in contrast to Dan, has performed the work of mediated labour. He has been patient and hardworking along the whole journey; in fact, at each stop along the way, Ben has focused on the building of a secure, containing home. He thus has not rushed headlong for the pleasure of the big payoff which will magically bring happiness. Yet, in the end, Ben hopes that this mediating work will secure the fortune, a fortune of gold that will bring light to the darkness. Is this then the essence of a northern masculinity, that northern men will build and work and toil with a focus on the fortune, the truth that awaits them at the end of the journey?

Lou, on the other hand, says to Ben, "We don't need this gold." (272) Why is Lou giving up the quest for gold? Why has she now aligned herself with Gussie Meadows, stepping out of the tracks, no longer focusing on the fabulous fortune at the end of the trail that will bring that long-awaited access to the pleasure of the real? Lou explains that she and Peek have saved a lot of money through their work at the Malamute Saloon. They, like Ben, have laboured hard, and their labour has brought incremental savings, built up over time. Now, because of those savings, they (Ben, Peek, and herself) could go back to Iowa and settle down, just as Gussie has returned to San Francisco with her savings. In her persistent plea to Ben, Lou emphasizes the aspect of home, in particular Ben's home in Iowa, his desire to settle down and take care of his mother. Lou tells Ben that, before this quest for gold, she has never really had a home, that Peek has never really had a home, nor a father, nor any proper schooling.

Ben will have nothing to do with this. It feels to him like someone has kicked him in the face. Ben's labour is fixated on the big payoff, enormous and monumental, not small change adding up into savings. With a manly pride, he is bound and determined to get the gold. It's not that he doesn't want those things that Lou talks about. Ben isn't Dan. Yet, Ben is driven by the idea that all the movements along the way that had established the security of home could only be meaningful if the end product was secured, the truth of gold that made everything meaningful, which would include the securing of home that comes afterward.

Herein lies the tragic yet beautiful truth of a northern masculinity. Men like Ben are heroes who slave away (unlike Dan, who remains in infancy). They work hard, they love, they build homes, they father, yet the quest that hardens their gaze and that makes all the other things meaningful is the quest for the pure substance. The tragedy here is that often these male heroes lack the realization that this quest for the pure substance is really a quest for love, a pure love, one that knows no bounds. This is part of the tragedy that befalls Ben.

After a hard winter, Ben finally returns to the Malamute Saloon carrying two heavy bags of gold. Dan is in his corner, playing cards, and once again, losing. In front of the scales where Lou is working, Ben lifts a gold nugget from his pocket, a nugget the size of a small brain – a golden brain. Lou fails at first to recognize Ben. When she does, there are two sacks of gold between them.

This in-betweenness has always been there. Gold has been the object of desire from the beginning. It has organized their quest, given it purpose, meaning. Now that Ben has struck gold, it could be said that he has what he has always been looking for. The impossible object of desire has been found. Lou announces to Ben that he is rich, twice over.

Yet, the sacks of gold are not what orient Ben's desire at this point. It is the nugget of gold that is important. Ben gives the nugget to Lou, "as if for all those weeks and months he had been looking for that one outstanding nugget to present to Lou as a gift." (282) How is this gift as a mediating element different from the fortune brought by the bags of gold? The nugget that is a golden brain can be contrasted to the state of Ben's face and head. Peek tells us that Ben's "face had frozen in spots. I could see the dead whiteness at the tip of his nose, on his cheeks above his whiskers. His eyes had gone back deep inside his skull." (283) We have an image here of a dead man, an empty skull, the life beaten out of it by the struggle of labour. The death drive has performed its emptying work. However, as soon as the skull is emptied, we discover that it has been filled again, now with a golden brain, a golden brain which has the ability to instantaneously transform deadness into life. As Ben offers the nugget to Lou he extends to his partner the gift of life, the golden brain that will overcome the will of death. To Ben, this is a sign of their bond.

Yet, Lou can't touch the nugget. She says to Ben, "keep it until we get to the cabin." (282) Peek's commentary on this is important. He tells us that, in delaying the acceptance of the gift from Ben, Lou "was talking about home. A homestake. She said cabin but she meant home." (282) For Lou, the gift of the gold nugget, as a sign of partnership, of bonding, can only be properly accepted in the context of the home that slowly and laboriously she and Ben and Peek have been constructing since they met on the boat. Gold as the ultimate object of desire that promises instantaneous renewal can only work its magic when set within the framework of the home that can contain its power. We could say that death rules unless gold appears, yet gold's appearance takes different forms of expression. In this instance, gold appears first as the gift of the nugget and second as the bags of gold. If the gift of the nugget confirms the intersubjective bond of Ben and Lou, then what of the bags of gold that Ben has hauled into the saloon and will need to be cashed out in relation to the contractual partnership he has with Dan?

According to the contract between Dan and Ben, half of the profits from the bags of gold will go to Dan. At this moment, sitting in his corner gambling table, Dan is out of debt. Peek tells us that Dan now has the opportunity to walk away from the table, collect his money, and head to San Francisco, to Gussie Meadows. In other words, Dan has the opportunity at this point to see the fruits of the contract go to the confirmation of love, his love for Gussie. Peek thinks love is the important thing, not the gold. The gold, the money, the riches, they mediate the bond, but are not the actual object of desire. The object of desire, in Peek's eyes, is the connection between the two subjects, not the individual and the gold. Dan thinks that he loves Gussie, yet he never really leaves his place of hiding – the barrel, the saloon, the gambling corner – to confirm his love for her. He remains solipsistically enclosed, thinking that access to the outside world, the world of love, can only come through access to a mysterious object – *das Ding* – which, it is hoped, will magically transform everything. Dan now has enough to get him to San Francisco and to Gussie, but he believes that this is not enough; he needs it all, all of the gold, to give him entry to love. He believes that nothing less than the all will bring him satisfaction.

This then becomes the downfall of the contract between Dan and Ben on Dan's part. The 50/50 deal is not on, perhaps has never been on for Dan, because Dan is a gambler in hiding. He wants all the gold and is willing to risk everything to get it. In his gambling corner, he plays the big one and loses everything. Hegg, the man he loses to, offers to play again. He loves fish and will bet all that Dan has just lost for the keg owned by Ben that sits on top of the piano and which both he and Dan believe to be full of fish. Dan says to Lou that Ben can have the whole sack of gold to himself if he gives Dan the barrel. Lou tells him he can have the barrel, but it's not full of fish, but whiskey. Hegg is a teetotaler, and Lou suggests to Dan that Hegg might not be happy with whiskey instead of fish. Dan's only option now is to go for the bag of gold, and to eliminate Ben.

The tragedy of the contract between Dan and Ben extends as well to Ben's desire. Despite the confirmation present through the gift of the nugget, Ben's desire is riddled with doubt. He is still not sure of Lou's love. In particular, he is jealous of the bond he perceives between Lou and Dan, believing their connection to be a sexual connection. Peek informs us that there has never been a sexual connection between Lou and Dan. The connection they did have was due to the fact that they both had been hiding and were, with the quest for gold, hoping that fortune would bring them out of hiding. Peek believes that this brought about a special kind of caring between them, that Lou cared for Dan as one who faced a common plight. Yet, their paths have diverged quite significantly, something that Ben, tragically, cannot recognize. Right from her coming out of hiding on the boat, Lou has established a partnership with Ben that has been continually built up as a loving bond and a loving home. She sees the gift of the nugget as confirmation of this love. But Ben now sustains a tragic misrecognition. Despite all of his past that has allowed him to be a man who works and loves, who labours to love, he falls for the trap of jealousy. Intersubjective mediation fades away for Ben, just as it had for Dan. He wants it all, wants it without question, without any intrusion by the other. Ben believes that Dan has come between him and Lou, and he seeks to get rid of Dan, and by doing so, get rid of the care (a type of love) that Lou has for Dan, the care his beloved other might have for the world apart from her devotion to him.

Ben sits down at the piano and begins to play something no one in the saloon had ever heard before. Peek says that his playing "got hold of all of us, and each of us, our skin and our bones. He got all the way in. And he started to claw and rip." (286) Ben has a hunger, a hunger for love. His playing moves to a crescendo. Peek says you could hear riverboats, arrivals and departures, "departures from home and then the returns." (288)

The expression of love in Ben's playing is all about home and the mother, the love of the mother. Nostalgia for the love of the mother, a melancholic mood that says that nothing compares to her love, not even the painstakingly established mutual love of Lou. Ben's melancholy finds its ultimate expression when he hits a chord which turns everybody in the saloon inside out and upside down, all of them suddenly confused. Everyone is squirming, becoming unhinged. Moreover, everyone starts holding on to each other, as if by clinging to someone they can face the experience of the abyss without the mother's love. The place becomes deadly still, except for Ben's playing. After the chaos of a motherless world, Ben returns to the mother's love, playing soft, making love the only way he knew, back home in Iowa, back in mommy's world.

Ben then stops playing and speaks: "One of you here is a hound of hell.... And that one is Dan McGrew." (294, 295) Then the shots start flying. Peek is the one who fires the first shot, having taken a six-shooter hidden in a saloon drawer. Peek shoots thinking he can bring peace. He wants to stop all the wanting between the men, between Dan and Ben. He wants them to accept the love they have, rather than have to go for an impossible love in relation to an impossible object. Peek aims at and hits the keg of whiskey sitting on top of the piano. He hopes that everyone will then relax and fill up on the whiskey that would pour out for all, just like the whiskey that had poured out at the big roundup party at Bennett City. As at other points in their trek, whiskey shows itself to be a desired mediating element that works differently from the sacks of gold that are destroying everything. If it is exchanged freely, it can bring people together. The shot Peek fires is a shot for a love that will situate people in the possibilities of satisfaction that lie before them, not a love that demands the impossible.

Peek's shot, however, does not have the desired effect. It only makes Ben hesitate with his gun, losing his rhythm, sending his first shot wide of its mark. At the same time, Dan has started firing his gun. Ben and Dan each fire three shots. The last two of Ben's go straight to Dan's heart, killing him. Two of Dan's shots are wild, but the third strikes. By this time Lou has sensed the disaster and has taken hold of Ben, thinking that Dan would then stop shooting. Dan's third shot goes through both Lou and Ben, killing them both.

Dan and Ben are men who display two different relationships to desire, the mother, and home. The question here is one of how desire accesses the outside world of meaning and fulfillment. In the story, this is figured as the quest for gold, gold being the object that can bring meaning and fulfillment. Dan is always seeking the magical solution to securing this object, a magical solution that is that of the master who doesn't labour over time for the object, but gambles that one stroke of this or that – the card game, the stake – can do the deed. In short, Dan has never really left the barrel; he remains immobile in the corner of the saloon, getting others to do the dirty work, gambling for the big payoff. His quest for love always leaves him lost for love, because the object of fulfillment is a phantom object, which disappears as easily as it appears. Dan seems to have preferred this quest for the impossible object over any mediated labour in the world outside the barrel, where love is secured through the work of building the home. Dan has no home except the barrel. He represents that type of masculinity that prefers the master-status of the barrel over the intersubjective network of home.

In contrast, Ben, throughout the story, chooses the work of building the home over the solipsism and narcissism of the barrel. From the shore, through Skagway, Dyee, Bennett City, and Dawson City, Ben works slowly and patiently for love, winning the trust of Lou and Ben, and each time securing an intersubjective space of recognition for himself. Even at the Eldorado Creek claim, Ben seems to embody a type of masculinity where hard labour in the belly of the earth-mother will, after some time, bring meaning and fulfillment. This is embodied in the discovery of the gold nugget. Ben goes into the belly of the mother, and finds the golden object of desire. He is awarded for his labours by a gift which must be given to the other. He moves from mother to partner and presents the gift-object to Lou as a sign of their intersubjective bond. In contrast to Dan, where there is no movement, no possibility of escape from the enveloping confines of the womb-barrel, Ben seems to be able move from mother to partner through the labour of love. In this movement, he has the possibility of recognition from an outside other who can confirm in love his identity. Dan, on the other hand, is lost in narcissism.

In one sense, Ben's story ends a tragic one, because instead of staying with the gift of the nugget – and leaving with Lou to go home – he allows himself to be consumed with the bags of gold and jealous desire. Ben knows that Lou has a connection with Dan, a caring brought about by a mutual past of hiding, and rather than seeing this as part of the experience of a partnership with an independent other who cares for others, Ben views this other line as a threat. He wants Lou to himself and Dan's intrusion, Dan as mediating element, brings forth a desire for aggressive attack, an attempt to eliminate the intrusion.

In another sense, however, this tragic element bound up with jealousy is partially overcome, because Ben dies in the arms of Lou and, at that moment, knows that his quest for gold has, in the end, discovered love.

After the long journey of Ben, Lou, and Peek seeking their fortune, Peek is left alone with the bags of gold, the claim out at Eldorado Creek, the house built for Gussie, and the management of the Malamute Saloon. Peek comments that although it might be true that we suffer and die, it is also true that we suffer and live. (299) Peek is the only one who survives unscathed, and it is left to him to bury the loved ones.

The three coffins for Ben, Lou, and Peek are placed side by side in the Dawson graveyard, but because the Klondike River (a tributary of the Yukon) floods in the spring, the whole graveyard washes away, floating down the Yukon.

We could say that this washing away of the coffins of Ben, Lou, and Dan affirms that all things wash away, because of the omnipresence of the death drive. The death drive has been an ever-present force in the Klondike Gold Rush, especially in relation to the building of homes, because homes were built and then taken down as the journey to Dawson proceeded. It could be argued that this final washing away establishes the central quality of impermanence to the quest for fortune. The attempt to grab hold of fortune, to find the bags of gold, is thwarted by the continual flow of the river, which washes away any permanent acquisition of the object of desire. Flowing river beats permanent earth. The flow cannot be contained by the solidity of earth. We might think that the fortune is there, but we are fools. The object of desire, the love we seek so desperately from the earth and from the mother and from home, cannot be acquired. It is an impossible object that is forever down the river, beyond our grasp.

Yet, this seeming triumph of the flowing river and the death drive over the permanence of the earth and the love of mother and home does not have the final say. It turns out that Peek has saved Lou's body from being washed away, from being sent down the flowing river. Peek has insisted throughout the journey that love will prevail, and he now is going to make sure that it will. He had put gravel in the coffin of Lou's that washed away, and while a three-day wake was being held for the dead at the Malamute Saloon (amply provided for by two leftover kegs of whiskey), Peek finds some private time to bury his mother. And so he begins to laboriously dig a hole under the cabin.

Ben had laboured in the belly of the earth to find the nugget of gold for Lou. This was the fortune that was discovered and confirmed the search for home and the search for love. Peek is now intent on preserving that fortune. As Ben did at the claim, he builds a fire of dried wood and heats the frozen ground so that it can be dug into to make room for the coffin. In the hole he digs, Peek makes a bed of spruce boughs and roses and places Lou's body on the soft bed. In her hands he places the gold nugget, the gift from Ben. He in effect returns the nugget of gold to its place in the earth, its place in the belly of the mother. Yet, this return to the mother is one that confirms and consolidates the love that was established between Ben and Lou, becoming the foundation, the ground, for the home that stands above it, where Ben and Lou were to live, and where Peek will live out his life.

Peek stays true to his mother, and true to the mother's love. And he knows that, in the end, this fidelity is all about holding on to each other and to affirming our partnerships. Peek tells us that we "must learn to hold each other." (307) And he wants to continue "to join two partners who, once they were together, were never really apart again." (307) The constant work of the death drive does not rule. Its insistent unravelling does not have the final say. Rather, the fortune discovered by Ben, Lou, and Peek announces that the victory goes to love, to the abiding work of home and partnership.

CONCLUSION

One of the central arguments in this work has been that the uniqueness of northern love lies principally in a unique struggle with the love of the father and the love of the mother. In terms of what this might say about possible features of Canadian masculinity, perhaps we could say that the relationship to the Canadian frontier differentiates itself from the American experience of the frontier by pointing North rather than West. Northern males, at least northern males who can be said to be heroes, do not flee the domesticated mother to identify with a powerful, undomesticated father, but remain tied to the mother's love and from that base negotiate a relationship to the father and his love.

This return of the northern male to the mother and the unique bond that dominates that return raises an important theoretical question that has preoccupied this work. The persistent question has been whether the trauma of the father that is experienced by Hood (in Wiebe's novel) and Peek (in Kroetsch's novel) leads to a regressive return to the mother. In other words, to put it in more precise psychoanalytic language, does remaining steadfast in the mother's love point to the lack of a strong paternal function, a lack of that paternal force that can lead the young boy out into the exciting activity of the outside world? Does this mean that northern males, like Hood and Peek, miss out on the pleasures of an aggressive, active masculinity, traditionally associated with the oedipal father?

The answer to this question that I have provided is that, although there are not, in Wiebe and Kroetsch's novels, strong depictions of oedipal fathers, there is the strong presence of imaginary fathers. In other words, when we are able to distinguish between two kinds of paternal presence, we can see that a lack of a strong oedipal father does not mean a lack of the father altogether.

In order to flesh this insight out a bit more in this conclusion, I would like to focus once again on the love experienced by two principal characters in the novels, Hood and Peek. I want to especially concentrate on the role the father plays in each of their lives, and how that intersects with each of their relationships with their mothers. Both Hood and Peek experience distress and anxiety about fathers who were, in their own distinct ways, absent in providing a source of identification for them. How did this absence unfold in each case and how did it initiate a unique return to the mother and her love?

<hr/>

First, Hood. We know that while Hood is dying out on the barrens he hallucinates his father's voice and that the experience of that voice is traumatic. Hood returns in memory to childlike vulnerability and pictures the father not as a keeper of that vulnerability, but as a violator of it. Hood's memory is of a father who did not entice his son out of vulnerability into a confident, active subjectivity. Instead, his father has taken on a condemning voice that sounds like the voice of God to Job. He insistently hounds Hood, forever leaving a guilty, trembling, passive subject.

I have argued that Hood, like Job, can be seen as a subject who is sacrificed for the sins of the father. In essence, he could be viewed as a scapegoat. Certainly, the idea of Job as scapegoat resonates for Hood, because it fits the particular memories he has of his father. Hood never moves to a position of reconciliation because there was no reconciliation with the father in his experience. And as he experiences abandonment on the barrens, he is returned to what feels like a foundational abandonment, the feeling of a young boy exceedingly vulnerable in the presence of an austere, distant father, a father who refused to cross the divide of vulnerability and provide a nurturing hand to lead his son forward.

The abandonment of Hood by his father speaks to the absence of the imaginary father. In one sense, Hood's father did take on one aspect of the oedipal task, namely, that of intervening in the mother-child dyad (for Hood was a mama's boy) and sending him out into the outside world, in this case, the hyper-masculine world of the British navy. However, what was missing in Hood's experience was the preparation for oedipal masculinity by the presence of an imaginary father who, prior to the instance of law and prohibition, could serve as an ideal figure of identification and thus serve as both like the mother (through the close bonds fostered by identification) and not like the mother (a distance from the maternal imago). Hood's austere Anglican father had no ability or desire to perform the role of imaginary father; nor did he want to fulfill the remaining oedipal tasks (beyond the cut itself and having to do with the struggle with law and prohibition), leaving those tasks to Franklin. This left Hood with a choice between the cold void of Franklin's masculinity and a return to the mother through his experience with Greenstockings in the maternal lodge. He chooses the latter and can only represent the former as a haunting presence.

Nonetheless, Hood's experience with Keskarrah and Greenstockings in the maternal lodge can be viewed as providing him with an experience of the imaginary father. Keskarrah, the shaman, who the English consider to be a feminized dreamer, teaches Hood how to draw properly. And it is in his encounter with the vital image as opposed to the abstract name that Hood is able to properly draw the things around him, especially Greenstockings. And as Greenstockings moves from mother to sister to lover, Hood is finally able to feel free and alive as a human, a feeling he could never gain in relation to his father or Franklin in their austere oedipal demands. Yet, despite this powerful relationship to the imaginary father, Hood, while dying on the barrens, is still haunted and traumatized by his experience of abandonment by his father back in England.

What about Peek? Peek shares with Hood the experience of being abandoned by the father. The difference is that while Hood knew his father, Peek did not, having no conscious memories of his father. And while Hood experiences his father in memory as traumatic, Peek is left with a vacant space that is filled by other figures who become figures of identification for him.

Certainly, Peek demonstrates a strong maternal connection. He is devoted to his mother, and that devotion structures his subsequent love and desire. Yet, what distinguishes Peek's experience is the presence of mediating figures who embody the mother's love while at the same time providing a lure to the exciting outside world. In effect, what Peek experiences is the mediating presence of the imaginary father. Peek encounters many figures who provide both the distancing lure of the paternal at the same time as the containing presence of maternal love. Gussie Meadows can be viewed this way, for Gussie, besides being Peek's lover (in a motherly way), is also his boss who teaches him the skills of work and shows him how to use a gun to protect himself.

It is in his relationship with Ben, though, that we see this unique paternal role of an imaginary father played out most dramatically. It is important, though, to note how Peek's openness to the paternal presence of Ben is made possible by his encounter with his father, J Badger. Peek's encounter with his father is structured by a parodic overturning. Peek's father is overturned through humour and laughter, and this clears out the paternal space for Peek so that he is open to new influences in that space. Peek finds his father frozen and stiff, after having died in an avalanche. One can't help but laugh in encountering J Badger, hunched over the back of a horse, hugging its rear end.

Ben is the figure who enters the paternal space just opened up. Ben becomes a stepfather to Peek, and provides for Peek a figure of identification from which he can accept the frailties of human action, as well as a model for love, work, and desire. And it is from the ground of this relationship to Ben that Peek learns about the ideals of partnership, home, and intersubjective recognition.

———•◦•———

On the basis of these concluding reflections on Hood and Peek, I would like to propose the figure of the imaginary father as the distinctive and exemplary figure of northern love. The uniqueness of northern love in contrast to western love (go North, not West) is that imaginary fathers play an ideal role in the construction of masculine identity. The imaginary father is a preparation for the work of the oedipal father, and this means that in northern love there is no demand that the masculine subject radically cut ties with maternal love. The imaginary father allows for a movement away from the maternal into a space that is like that of maternal love yet also unlike it, partaking in the pleasures of paternal distance. Maternal love and paternal distance are, in their intertwining, reflected in the strong and enduring presence of the imaginary father. It is in this way that Canadian masculinity can look to the imaginary father as the ideal figure of northern love.

REFERENCES

Atwood, Margaret. 1995. *Strange things: The malevolent North in Canadian Literature.* Oxford: Clarendon Press.

Benjamin, Jessica. 1994. "Shadow of the Other Subject," *Constellations* 1(2):, 231–54.

———— 1995. *Like Subjects, Love Objects: Essays on Recognition and Sexual Difference.* New Haven: Yale University Press.

Bosso, Matthew, Laura McCall, and Dee Garceau, eds. 2001. *Across the Great Divide: Cultures of Manhood in the American West.* New York: Routledge.

Butler, Judith. 1993. "Arguing With the Real," in *Bodies That Matter: The Discursive Limits of "Sex."* New York: Routledge. Pp. 187–222.

———— 1997. *The Psychic Life of Power: Theories in Subjection.* Palo Alto, CA: Stanford University Press.

———— 2000. *Antigone's Claim: Kinship between Life and Death.* New York: Columbia University Press.

Davis, Ann. 1982. *A Distant Harmony: Comparisons in the Painting of Canada and the United States of America.* Winnipeg: Winnipeg Art Gallery.

Dean, Tim. 2000. *Beyond Sexuality.* Chicago: University of Chicago Press.

Dews, Peter. 1995. "The Tremor of Reflection," in *The Limits of Disenchantment: Essays on Contemporary European Philosophy.* London: Verso.

Fink, Bruce. 1995. *The Lacanian Subject: Between Language and Jouissance.* Princeton, NJ: Princeton University Press.

Frye, Northrop. 1971. *The Bush Garden: Essays on the Canadian Imagination.* Toronto: Anansi Press.

Grace, Sherrill E. 2002. *Canada and the Idea of North.* Kingston, ON: McGill-Queen's University Press.

Girard, René. 1987. *Job: The Victim of His People*. London: Athlone Press.

Hegel, G. W. F. 1981. *Philosophy of Right*. Trans. with Notes, T. M. Knox. Oxford: Oxford University Press.

———— 1991. *The Encylopaedia Logic: Part 1*. Trans. with Intro and Notes, T. F. Geraets et al. Indianapolis: Hackett Publishing Co.

Kimmel, Michael. 1996. *Manhood in America: A Cultural History*. New York: The Free Press.

Kristeva, Julia. 1987. "Freud and Love," in *Tales of Love*. Trans. Leon S. Roudiez. New York: Columbia University Press.

———— 2000. *The Sense and Non-Sense of Revolt: The Powers and Limits of Psychoanalysis*. Trans. Jeanine Herman. New York: Columbia University Press.

———— 2002. *Intimate Revolt: The Powers and Limits of Psychoanalysis*. Trans. Jeanine Herman. New York: Columbia University Press.

Kroetsch, Robert. 1995. "Why I Went Up North and What He Found When He Got There," in *A Likely Story: The Writing Life*. Red Deer, AB: Red Deer College Press. Pp. 13–40.

———— 1998. *The Man from the Creeks*. Toronto: Vintage Canada.

Lacan, Jacques. 2002. *Ecrits: A Selection*. Trans. Bruce Fink. New York: W. W. Norton.

Mitcham, Allison, 1983. *The Northern Imagination: A Study of Northern Canadian Literature*. Moonbeam, ON: Penumbra Press.

Northey, Margot. 1976. *The Haunted Wilderness: The Gothic and Grotesque in Canadian Fiction*. Toronto: University of Toronto Press.

Reynolds, Stephen. 2001. Private email correspondence with Assistant Professor of Systematic Theology at Trinity College, University of Toronto.

Saul, John Ralston. 1997. *Reflections of a Siamese Twin: Canada at the End of the Twentieth Century*. Toronto: Viking.

Savran, David. 1998. *Taking It Like a Man: White Masculinity, Masochism and Contemporary American Culture*. Princeton, NJ: Princeton University Press.

Silverman, Kaja. 1992. "Masochism and Male Subjectivity," in *Male Subjectivity at the Margins*. New York: Routledge.

———— 2000. *World Spectators*. Palo Alto, CA: Stanford University Press.

Theunissen, Michael. 1991. "The Repressed Intersubjectivity in Hegel's *Philosophy of Right*," in *Hegel and Legal Theory*, edited by Drucilla Cornell et al. New York: Routledge. Pp. 3–63.

Tiefensee, Dianne. 1994. *The Old Dualities: Deconstructing Robert Kroetsch and His Critics*. Kingston, ON: McGill-Queen's University Press.

Wiebe, Rudy, 1989. *Playing Dead: A Contemplation Concerning the Arctic.* Edmonton, AB: NeWest Press.

———— 1994. *A Discovery of Strangers.* Toronto: Vintage Canada.

Žižek, Slavoj. 1989. *The Sublime Object of Ideology.* New York: Verso.

———— 1992. *Enjoy Your Symptom! Jacques Lacan in Hollywood and Out.* New York: Routledge.

———— 1993. *Tarrying With the Negative: Kant, Hegel and the Critique of Ideology.* Durham, NC: Duke University Press.

———— 1996. "I Hear You With My Eyes or The Invisible Master," in *Gaze and Voice as Love Objects,* edited by Renata Saleci and Slavoj Žižek. Durham, NC: Duke University Press. Pp. 90–126.

———— 2002. *The Fragile Absolute Or, Why Is the Christian Legacy Worth Fighting For?* New York: Verso Press.

INDEX